MW00779906

THE DECEIVING OF THE BLACK RACE

◇

By

MOSES FARRAR

Biblical Historian & Researcher

MONÄMI PUBLICATIONS
PHILADELPHIA, PENNSYLVANIA

Website: mosesfarrar.com

Copyright © 1996, 2012 by Moses Farrar

TWELFTH PRINTING

Printed in the United States of America

REVISED EDITION, 2012

ii

DEDICATIONS

To My Beloved Mother
the Late SAINT LAVINIA FARRAR
(godly, pious, refined, intelligent)

To THREE GREAT RABBIS: MY MENTORS

To the Late
ELDER EDWARD and SAINT BERTHA SUYDAM
My childhood mentors in the Printing Trade

To My GREAT SON, "REGGIE"
"Tho' he be dead, he yet speaketh, . . ."
through his music!

To My Deceased Siblings
CLARENCE, MARIE, INEZ, REGINALD, CLIFTON

TABLE OF CONTENTS

v

PREFACE

THIS BOOK is written from biblical and historical perspectives, and brings to light many unpopular, neglected and hidden truths. For too long a time the Black race has been ill-depicted and cited by many as not ever having had a culture and not having made any contributions to civilization. This work in many places denounces and seeks to undo, through undeniable facts, that type of thinking. However, the main purpose of this book is for the impartation of Truth – a truth that has been hidden, crushed and nearly destroyed for more than twenty centuries.

THE DECEIVING OF THE BLACK RACE is written for people of all races, nationalities and religious persuasions, but mainly it is out of genuine love and concern for my people which have compelled me to put in print many facts that may serve to raise the self-esteem of those of that most hated race. It is hoped that this book will additionally help in the accomplishment of the following: (1) providing of a better understanding of the Bible and Bible-related history, and (2) uncovering of the deceits and untruths that have engulfed the nations almost globally for more than 2,000 years.

THE OBJECT OF THIS BOOK IS NOT TO OFFEND, BUT TO ENLIGHTEN.

It is not the intention of the author to convey in any way the superiority of those of African ancestry or the inferiority of those of European extraction, neither is it my intent to promote any racial or prejudicial point of view. I believe that no one has a monopoly on the Almighty, and the truths which He has revealed to His prophets are for all peoples.

I have sought in this book to tackle some of the tough

topics of the Bible and its related history, which many authors – past and present – have evaded. The Bible is often difficult to understand, therefore many read only those easy-to-comprehend passages such as certain portions of the Psalms, the Gospels, and the Epistles of Paul. However, there is great wisdom, promise and power in the messages contained in The Law and The Prophets. This book will acquaint the reader with many unfamiliar yet beautiful Old Testament scriptural passages and, through the interpretations herein provided, will help to broaden one's awareness of the Creator.

What I have termed as a "teaching style" has been adopted for this book, hence the frequent use of parentheses, brackets and dashes, all for the sake of clarity.

As often as possible, when reading this book the Bible should be opened so that the reader may note or highlight the various passages to which the author refers. I have quoted for the most part from the King James Version of the Bible; where there were discrepancies, however, the Hebrew Scriptures (English translation) is used. The terms "Old Testament" and "New Testament" have been employed many times in this work, but such terminologies are really misnomers. Their proper designations are "Hebrew Scriptures" (for O.T.) and "Greek Scriptures" (for N.T.). The Hebrew Scriptures are also known as The Holy Scriptures. However, for the sake of convenience the terms "Old Testament" and "New Testament" will be used interchangeably with "the Hebrew Scriptures."

Where other authors have been quoted verbatim in this book, I have made sure that I have either obtained their per-mission, or have made certain that their works are in the realm of public domain.

It is with great pleasure that I make a few acknowledg-ments. First and foremost I thank the Almighty and Most High

Creator for His manifold blessings in enabling me to undertake and complete this gigantic task which has been like a "fire shut up in my bones" for many a year.

Other acknowledgments are to: Lacy Gordon Blair, M.D., a dear friend and Israelite brother of New York City, for his never-ending encouragement and support in my seminars for more than 15 years; Ella Hughley, MSW and author; Leora Neal, MSW, CSW, and Eunice Turner, M.Ed., all Israelite sister of Queens, Bronx, and Brooklyn, NY, respectively, for their great encouragement and assistance in brainstorming and researching since 1981; my sister, Mary Farrar-Jones, and my brother, Clifton C., for their loving and understanding spirit toward me – their baby brother – in this endeavor.

Last, but not least, special thanks to my wonderful children – Muriel, Valerie, Regina, Benjamin, Miriam, Monique and Lisa – for the mutual love and respect that abound between us.

Please do not just *Read* this book,

but rather, vigorously and energetically

Study it!

Chapter 1

THE BIBLE:
A 'BLACK HISTORY' BOOK

WE HAVE BEEN BLESSED BY THE CREATOR to have done research on the nations of antiquity recorded in Holy Scriptures.
To aid in this research were several versions of the
encyclopedia, a collegiate dictionary, various Bible diction-
aries and commentaries, and many versions of the Bible,
including one with a chain reference. We have also read the
works of a few great historians and other writers – some
Black, some White – among them, the late J. A. Rogers,
Professor Joseph P. Williams, Dr. Yosef ben Yechanan, Dr.
John Henric Clark, Dr. Ivan Van Sertima, Professor Rudolph
Yehuda Windsor, Steven S. Jacobs, and others.

From the foregoing sources as well as from additional ones
we have concluded that of the scores of nations mentioned in
the Old Testament, almost all of them were of the Black race.
These nations include, but are not limited to, the Ethiopians,
the Egyptians, the Babylonians, the Assyrians, the entire
Canaanite family of nations, the Hebrews/Israelites, the
Ishmaelites, and many others.

The Bible – though not perfect – is the "book of books," is
still the world's best seller, and is our main source of
information. It contans history, prose poetry, psalms,
proverbs, romance industry, myths, fables, prophecy, revelation, riddles and much more. Covering a span of nearly 4,500
years, the Bible is truly a one-of-a-kind treasure.

11

Let us now engage in an indepth study of portions of the tenth, eleventh and twelfth chapters of Genesis, with the cross-referencing of other scriptures, and intersperse that study with some facts from the pages of secular history to identify the ethnic classification of the aforementioned nations.

After the Flood it was left to the sons of Noah – Shem, Ham and Japheth – and their wives to repopulate the world. Genesis 9:18, 19 states, *"And the sons of Noah, that went forth of the ark, were Shem, and Ham, and Japheth: and Ham is the father of Canaan. These are the sons of Noah: and of them was the whole earth overspread."*

Archeologists, anthropologists and historians – biblical and non-biblical – agree that all the races of mankind which have evolved within the last 4,700 years fall under the racial classifications of Semitic (Shem), Hamitic, or Japhetic.

Of Noah's sons, Japheth and his descendants are the first mentioned in the tenth chapter of Genesis (vss. 1-4). Originally, Japheth and his offspring were of the Black race, but after their migration to the Caucasus regions of Europe where the climate is foggy and cold and there is less sunshine, over the centuries they became lighter and lighter in complexion. A Caucasian race developed as a result. William Boyd in researching the genetics and races of man, states: *"We should find the blackest skins amongst men in the hottest parts of the world with strong sun. In the very cold part of the world further away from the equator with less sunshine, we find lighter skins among men."*

Both the 1871 (no error, 1871) and the 1986 editions of Smith's Bible Dictionary give the region where the Japheth-ites settled. From the 1871 edition: "JAPHETH *(extent)* Second son of Noah (Gen. 10:2, 6). YAPHAH *(fair)* may be the root-word, in allusion to the light complexion of the people of the Japhetic races who occupied the Isles of Greece (shores) and islands), coasts of the Great Sea (Mediterranean), and Asia Minor, Asia and Europe." From the 1986 edition: "Japheth *(enlargement)*. One of the three sons of Noah. The descendants of Japheth occupied the 'isles of the Gentiles,' Gen. 10:5 – i.e., the coast lands of the Mediterranean Sea in Europe and Asia Minor. – whence they spread abroad north-ward across the whole continent of Europe and a considerable portion of Asia."

Only four verses are devoted to Japheth in Genesis 10 (vss. 2-5), and his descendants are referred to as Gentiles, but never are the Shemites or Hamites so designated.

Our major emphases in this chapter will be on Shem and Ham, the progenitors of the Black race, and it will be pointed out how that the posterity of both these patriarchs – the Ham-ites of the Ethiopian, Egyptian, Babylonian, and Canaanite strains, and the Shemites of the Hebrew-Israelite strain – often dwelled together and intermingled as the same race of people, though each was of a different progenitor.

Ham had four sons: Cush, Mizraim, Phut, and Canaan, and each of them settled a country: Cush, Ethiopia; Mizraim, Egypt; Phut, Libya; and Canaan, the Land of Canaan (Gen. 10:6-20). Actually, it was not until circa 332 B.C.E., when the Greeks under Alexander the Great invaded Africa that they (the Greeks) changed the name of the country Cush to "Ethiopia" (which in Greek means *"burnt, black faces"*), and changed the name of the country Mizraim (originally known secularly as "Kemet," or "Chem") to "Egypt." These two countries – Ethiopia and Egypt – were known only as "Cush" and "Mizraim" (or "Kemet") for more than 3,800 years before the Greek infiltration.

The Hamites settled in Africa, and also sent many

branches into Asia; the Canaanites inhabited that region of Asia known as Palestine.

One may ask, How is it that the name "Ethiopia" appears in the Bible as early as the second chapter of Genesis, if the name was changed? The answer is, After the Greeks conquered the known world in the fourth century B.C.E., many biblical names were changed, including some names for the books of the Bible, to conform to the Greek influence. The names for the first five books as we know them – Genesis, Exodus, Leviticus, Numbers, and Deuteronomy – come out of Greece. The original Hebrew names for these books were: "BERESHIT" *(Genesis,* which means "in the beginning"); "SHEMOT" *(Exodus,* means "names" – v. 1: "These...names"); "VAYIKRA" *(Leviticus,* "and He called," from the first words of the text; "BEMIDBAR" *(Numbers,* "in the wilderness"): "DEBARIM" *(Deuteronomy,* "Words").

Hamites Establish 4 of the Greatest Civilizations Ever

Of all of the civilizations that have ever existed since the dawn of recorded history, none have excelled those of Ethiopia, Egypt, Babylon, and Assyria, all of which are Hamitic in origin.

ETHIOPIA *(burnt).* The country called in Hebrew CUSH: south of Egypt, from Syene (Eze. 29:10). The Hebrews traded with the Ethiopians (Isa. 45:14) in ebony, ivory, frankincense, gold and precious stones (Job 28:19). Settled by a Hamitic race (Gen. 10:6); dark (Jer. 13:23); men of stature (Isa. 18:2), fine-looking (Isa.38:7). The Sabaens were the most noted tribe.

EGYPT *(the black country).* It would be interesting and valuable if we could give here a full account of all the monuments which confirm scripture, found in Egypt; but as that would fill a large volume, we must admit only a few illustrations. The principal point illustrated by evidence derived from Egypt is the fact that Egypt was then a rich, powerful, and civilized nation. The name on the monuments is KEM *(black).* Called the land of Ham (Psa. 78:51; 105:23, 27; 106:21, 22).

BABYLON *(confusion).* The kingdom of Babylon comprised originally only an area of about 30,000 square miles, situated in the lowlands around and between the Euphrates and the Tigris, and south of Assyria. It was noted for its subtle wisdom, commercial eagerness, and military valor. Babylonian civilization was very old, dating beyond 2600 B.C.E.

ASSYRIA. Country on the Tigris, the capital of which was Nineveh. Named from Asshur, of the seed of Cush (Gen. 10:10-11). The mounds are the only relics of antiquity, and these contain (in those of Nineveh, and others recently explored by Layard), proofs of their greatness, in sculptures, inscriptions, and remnants of architecture. During the last forty years excavations about Nineveh have shown that they were possessed of a civilization which in many respects surpassed even that of Egypt. Nineveh is one of the largest cities that ever existed.

Neither the Bible nor any of the resource material at our disposal reveals any contributions whatsoever which the ancient Japhethites have made to world civilization. All that seems to be recorded of them is their family tree and the regions of their settlements. The Hamitic contributions, on the other hand, have been legion, as we have already seen. As for the Shemitic lineage, it gave to the world, through Abram (Abraham) – after ten generations of idolatry – the knowledge of the True and Living Divine Being, and since that time the awareness of His existence among men has never again ceased in the earth. The second most important contribution made by the Black descendants of Abraham was their gift of the Holy Scriptures (the Bible) to the world – a literary masterpiece!

One Branch of Shem Settles in Mesha

Five generations of one of the branches of Shem are mentioned in Genesis 10:22-25. Only one of Shem's seed of this branch, his great-great-great-great grandson, Joktan – and his 13 sons – is given the geographical location of "Mesha, as thou goest unto Sephar, a mount on the east" (Gen. 10:26-30). History pinpoints that location as "from near the Persian Gulf southwest, nearly across Arabia." None of the other offspring of Shem listed in Genesis 11:19-23 is given a land designation.

Another Branch of Shem Dwells with the Hamites

Terah, the father of Abram, became the patriarch of new generations. Although descended from Shem, they were all born in Hamitic territory, Ur of the Chaldees (11:27-30). Chaldea is the same country as Babylonia, the capital city of which is Babylon, built by Nimrod, grandson of Ham, (10:10).

After the death of his father and one of his two brothers, Abram gathered together all who had been born in Ur, and headed toward the country of Canaan, but stopped on the way at the city of Haran, dwelling there for a season (11:31). At age 75, Abram, with all his souls and substance, left Haran and journeyed to Canaan (12:4,5), a land settled by the Canaanites who were descendants of Ham (10:15-18). When famine ravaged Canaan, Abram, his family and servants took refuge in Egypt, "the land of Ham."

Over in the book of the prophet Ezekiel, God identifies the Israelites as having sprung from the Hamitic line. In Ezekiel

16:1-3, the following words are recorded:

"Again the word of the LORD came unto me, saying, Son of man, cause Jerusalem to know her abominations, and say, Thus saith the LORD God unto Jerusalem; Thy birth and thy nativity is of the land of Canaan; thy father was an Amorite and thy mother a Hitite." Jerusalem was the Holy City of the Israelites. Both the Amorite and the Hitite were descended from the man Canaan who was a descendant of Ham. The above scripture undeniably makes a definite Hamitic-Israelite connection.

Isaac, Jacob, the 12 tribes of Israel, and all the prophets from Moses through Jesus were of the seed of Abraham and were of the Black race.

It has already been established in this chapter that the ancient Egyptians were of the Black race. To prove that Moses was also a Black man, let us consider the following:

The story of the baby Moses' discovery by Pharoah's daughter is so well known that we need not tell it in its entirety. She recognized him as a Hebrew child from the blanket in which he was wrapped and the type of ark in which the baby lay, which differed from the Egyptian types. The princess reared Moses as her own son, with his biological mother, Jochebed (unbeknown to the royalty of the palace), as his nurse. **Moses must have greatly resembled the Egyptians in order for him to have "passed" as Pharoah's grandson for forty years.** Black Egyptians enslaved Black Israelites, just as White Germans exterminated White Jews during the Holocaust.

After Moses fled from Egypt to the land of Midian, he soon met the daughters of Reuel (also known as Jethro). Moses is called "an Egyptian" by the women (Ex. 2:19).

Time and space would fail us to tell the biblical story in its entirety of how Moses' hand miraculously turned white after placing it into his bosom (4:6, 7), or how that his sister Miriam was stricken with leprosy and was temporarily turned white; the point being that if they were already white, then where is the great wonder!

Some say it makes no difference the race of Abraham, Moses, Isaiah, Jeremiah, Jesus or the people of biblical times. Well, we say to that: It must make a difference, else the Whites in power over the last 2000 or more years would have kept all the paintings, portraits and pictures of the ancient peoples Black, as they were originally. If color makes no difference to the Caucasian race, then Napoleon Bonaparte would not have blown off the broad noses and thick lips of the ancient statues of Egypt. Try convincing them that color makes no difference. Open the average Bible, then write the publishers and tell them that in their next edition, please make all the pictures of the various characters as Black people, and see if it makes any difference to them.

Many Older Caucasian Jews Acknowledge
The African-Asian Origin of the Original Israelites

While living in Philadelphia before, for the last eight years of my residency there, my next-door neighbors were a Jewish couple seemingly between 75 and 80 years old. The wife's brother, also quite aged, would come to visit the couple each year from Florida. As the three of them sat on their porch one Saturday afternoon as I was returning from Sabbath services, my two daughters, they and I engaged in conversation. Upon learning that we were adherents of the Judaic faith, the Florida in-laws said to me, "You know, the original Jews were Black people."

Upon moving to Brooklyn in 1976, I met many, many Jews several years my senior – including an auctioneer from Chicago – also agreed that the Jews of biblical times were of the Black race. The chairman of the History Department of a Brooklyn college asked me five times before I consented, to do a lecture at that college. He chose the topic, *"Were the Original Jews Black?"* He also had posters for the lecture distributed in advance all over the college campus.

And lastly, since I've been in Rochester, NY (as of October 1993), a European Jew in his early 80s has made a very startling statement to me. It happened as we were engaged in a one-on-one conversation about B'nai Yisrael (Sons of Israel), the Black Israelites of Ethiopia. This Jewish gentleman said to me after a brief dialogue, *". . . Many Jews believe that Moses was Black!"*

I close this chapter with seven powerful words: "AWAKE, BLACK MAN, AND RECLAIM YOUR LEGACY!"

WE HAVE BEEN GREATLY DECEIVED!

Chapter 2

THE NICENE COUNCIL OF 325 A.D.:
Its Impact Upon the Sabbath,
& the Effects of Its Endorsement
of the Divinity of Jesus

THE STATISTICS LISTED ON THIS PAGE IN EARLIER PRINTINGS ARE NO LONGER VALID. They were correct at the writing of this book in 1995. The numbers have changed since then, so we offer an update on the figures, but not in the form of a chart, as before. We regret that the categorical breakdown is not now available. **What we *do* know, however, is that <u>there are currently 2.1 billion Christians worldwide.</u>**

World population has already reached 7,000,000,000 (seven billion), with Christianity numbering not even one-third of that total. Most Christians regard Sunday, the first day of the week universally, as the Lord's Day and/or the Christian Sabbath. Yet the masses among Sunday adherents are unaware of the truth of how the first day of the week became a so-called holy day, or how it came to be that Jesus is prayed to, worshipped and deified.

There are some Christian churches, however, which observe Saturday, the seventh day of the week universally, as God's holy Sabbath. These religious bodies include Seventh-Day Adventists, the Worldwide Church of God, Seventh-Day Baptists, and a few Pentecostal, or Apostolic groups. There are also some break-away factions of the aforementioned churches, such as the Church of God Seventh Day, which still hold to the biblical Sabbath.

These churches, though they embrace the original Sabbath as a part of their doctrine, still contend that Jesus was more than 'just human.' These Christian Sabbath-keeping groups, along with all of the rest of Christendom, are greatly divided as to who Jesus really was (or is, as they say), as well as on the doctrine of the Trinity. Their belief runs from *Jesus the Son of God,* to *Jesus as God Himself,* to *Jesus as co-Creator of the universe with God,* to *Jesus as Saviour of the world,* to *Jesus the Suffering Servant of Isaiah chapter 53.* The Unitarian Church, whose membership numbers in the millions, as well as thousands among some Pentecostals and others, do not believe in the doctrine of the Trinity.

The Apostle Paul and hundreds of pagan and Christian writers since him, whether willfully or ignorantly, have committed two evils: First, they have ravaged the sacred Old Testament Scriptures, systematically extracting from them a multitude of passages (which they have taken entirely out of content), and have applied them to Jesus. And secondly, they have succeeded in coercing and forcing millions into believing that Jesus was, and still is, equal with or greater than the Almighty and Most High God. Thus they have preyed upon and deceived the ignorant, for generations untold. Fear, hell and damnation, threats of fire and brimstone and even the death sentence itself has been pronounced upon millions over the centuries who refused to conform. (The out-of-context Scriptural passages referred to above will be outlined in detail elsewhere in this book in the chapter entitled *Alleged Christological References in Scripture.)*

Remember, when you rule the world you can do anything you want to do. And thus did the Greco-Roman Empire and the Roman Catholic Church, as we shall see in the startling, fully documented account that follows.

IT ALL HAPPENED SO LONG AGO

The Nicene Council, or, the Council of Nicæa, or, the Council of Níce (pronounced "neece") – all one and the same – was convened and presided over by Constantine the Great, Emperor of Rome, at Byzantine, Asia Minor, in the year 325 C.E. (A.D.). The main purpose of the Council's meeting, according to the Encyclopædia Britannica, the World Almanac of 1965, and many other sources, was to define Orthodox Christian beliefs. These beliefs included, but were not limited to, the Divinity of Christ, the Holy Trinity, and the dates of Christmas and Easter. The Nicene Creed, which was later revised and became known as the Apostles' Creed, was also an outgrowth of the Nicene Council The number one and most important item on the Council's agenda was the Arian Controversy, and next, the "Sunday Law" and the date of Easter.

The particular topic presently under discussion is in two parts: First, the Nicene Council's impact upon the God-given holy Sabbath; and second, the Council's endorsement of Jesus' divinity.

Let us now enter into a brief discourse on the "Change of the Sabbath." The Catholic Church, through its various church councils, changed the Sabbath from Saturday to Sunday, prior to the convening of the Council of Nice of 325. It was not a formal, but a gradual and almost unconscious transference of the one day to the other" (F. W. Farrar, *The Voice From Sinai,* p. 167). **(Farrar above not related to author of this book.)**

Sunday observance originated as a voluntary celebration of the resurrection, a custom without pretense of Divine authority.

"Opposition to Judaism introduced the particular festival of Sunday very early, indeed, into the place of the Sabbath. Perhaps at the end of the second century a false application of this kind had begun to take place, for men appear by that time to have considered laboring on Sunday a sin" (Augustus Neander, *The History of the Christian Religion,* p. 186). The observance of Sunday was at first <u>supplemental</u> to that of the Sabbath, <u>but in proportion as the gulf between the Church and the synagogue widened,</u> the Sabbath became less and less important and ended at length in being entirely neglected.

The following quotations are from some of the foremost Catholic publications:

"The Catholic Church, . . . by virtue of her divine mission, chamged the day from Saturday to Sunday" (The Catholic Morror, official organ of Cardinal Gibbons, Sept. 23, 1893).

"Is Saturday the 7th day according to the Bible and the Ten Commandments?

"I answer *yes!*

"Is Sunday the first day of the week and did the Church change the day – Saturday – for Sunday, the 1st day?

"I answer *yes!*

"Did Christ change the day?

"I answer *no!* Faithfully yours,

    J. Card. Gibbons."

"Ques. - Which day is the Sabbath day?

"Ans. - Saturday is the Sabbath day.

"Ques. - Why do we observe Sunday instead of Saturday?

"Ans. - We observe Sunday instead of Saturday because the Catholic Church transferred the solemnity from Saturday to Sunday" (Peter Geiermann, *The Convert's Catechism of Catholic Doctrine,* p. 50).

So we see over and over again that it was the Catholic Church that was initially responsible for the change of the Sabbath, and not, at first, Constantine the Great.

Church and State by this time had become one, however,

and in keeping with the Church's wishes, Emperor Constantine on March 7, 321 C.E. (A.D.), issued the first <u>civil legislation</u> proclaiming Sunday – the venerable Day of the Sun – a day of rest. For he said, <u>"Let us then have nothing in common with the detestable Jewish crowd"</u> (Eusebius, *The Life of Constantine,* Book 3, chapter 8).

The earliest recognition of the observance of Sunday as a <u>legal duty</u> is a constitution of Constantine in 325 A.D., enacting that all courts of justice, inhabitants of towns, and workshops were to be at rest on Sunday (the venerable Day of the Sun), with an exception in favor of those engaged in agricultural labor" (Encyclopædia Britannica).

The Emperor's proclamation read as follows:

"On the venerable Day of the Sun let the magistrates and people residing in cities rest, and let all workshops be closed. In the country, however, persons engaged in agriculture may freely and lawfully continue their pursuits, because it often happens that another day is not suitable for grain-sowing or vine-planting, lest by neglecting the proper moment for such operations the bounty of heaven should be lost. (Given the 7th day of March, 321." (Translated in *History of the Christian Church,* by Philip Schaff, Scribner's 1902 ed., Vol. 3, p. 380.)

<u>This edict, issued by Constantine, who first opened the way for the union of church and state in the Roman Empire,</u> in a manner supplied the lack of a divine command for Sunday observance. It was one of the important steps in <u>legally</u> bringing about the change of the Sabbath. The Council of Nice, A.D. 325, notices Sunday as a rest day incidentally as <u>already an old institution,</u> and makes some rules concerning the posture of worshippers.

Rome was the world power of the time, and whatever countries she dominated and conquered, she imposed upon

upon them her laws and spiritual doctrines. All religious institutions and individuals, therefore, which regard Sunday as a holy day or as the Lord's Day, are obeying the authority of the Catholic Church and Roman Empire. Truly, the impact of their influence over the past near-2000 years has been felt nearly around the globe.

****

Let us now move into the second and final part of our discussion: "The Effects of the Nicene Council's Endorsement of the Divinity of Jesus."

The Arian controversy, mentioned in the opening statement, was the most important item on the Council's agenda. And just what was the Arian controversy? Simply this: "Was Jesus human or divine?" (There was a member of the Council named Arius; hence the Arian controversy.)

Much of the Pauline Doctrine (the doctrine of the Apostle Paul (A.D. 35-A.D. 64) had already laid the groundwork for Gentile belief in Jesus as "Lord" and co-Creator of the universe (Ephesians 3:9 and Philippians 2:6, etc.).

Gerald Berry in his book, *Religions of the World,* published by Barnes and Noble, writes: "It remained for Saul, a Pharisee, a Roman-Jewish tentmaker of Tarsus, to rescue Christianity from the oblivion of other Messianic cults and give it a world meaning. At first he had persecuted the Nazarenes, but later he had been converted. Paul came to think of Jesus as a personal Redeemer, Saviour, or Lord, through whom he and all mankind could attain personal salvation.

"Jesus always remained a Jew [Israelite]; but Saul, the Jew, became Paul, the Christian founder. Where Jesus has been a prophet and a dreamer, Paul was a statesman, a builder and an organizer. Paul's religion took root in Antioch, where probably the <u>contemptuous term 'Christian'</u> was first used, but from the first it was a proselyting religion."

With the rise of the Catholic Church in the Second Century, the idea of the divinity of Jesus Christ was magnified more and more, reaching unto the Fourth Century, during which time the Council of Nicæa convened, in 325, to define Orthodox Christian beliefs.

Arius and those with him believed and stated that <u>Jesus was human, not divine.</u> Athanasius, another member of the Council, and those who sided with him proclaimed Jesus as divine. Arius' view was rejected, and he and his sympathizers were excommunicated from the Council. The Council then went on to <u>endorse the divinity of Jesus Christ,</u> issuing forth a document expressing confession of the Christian faith. The decree is known in history as the Nicene Creed, and reads as follows:

"I believe in one God, the Father Almighty, maker of heaven and earth, and of all things, visible and invisible;
And in one Lord Jesus Christ, the only begotten Son of God;
Begotten of the Father before all worlds, God of God, Light of Light, very God of very God; begotten, not made, being in one substance with the Father, through whom all things were made; who for us men and for our salvation came down from heaven, and was incarnate by the Holy Ghost of the Virgin Mary, and was made man, and was crucified also for us under Pontius Pilate; he suffered and was buried, and the third day he rose again according to the Scriptures, and ascended into heaven, and sitteth on the right hand of the Father; and he shall come again with glory, to judge the quick and the dead; whose kindgom shall have no end.
And I believe in the Holy Ghost, the Lord, the giver of life, who proceedeth from the Father and the Son, who with the Father and the Son together is worshipped and glorified, who spake by the prophets. And I believe in one holy catholic Church. I acknowledge one baptism for the remission of sins. And I look for the resurrection of the dead, and the life of the world to come. Amen.

The man whom the Greeks named *Iesous* ['Jesus'] and titled *Christos* ['Christ'] (whose Hebrew name was Yeshua ben Yosef), was a prophet of God, a great teacher, messenger and humanitarian; one who attained a state of righteousness and holiness, as each of us can – some possibly to greater or lesser degrees.

When Yeshua (Jesus) lived he regarded himself, and the people of his day who walked and talked with him, as well, regarded him as a prophet of God. There are scores of New Testament references, principally within the Gospels, which attest to his prophetship. A few of them follow:

Matthew 13:53-58; Matthew 21:11; Matthew 21:46; Mark 1:24 ("holy one of God"); Mark 6:15; Luke 7:16; 9:18-22 ("the Christ of God) (Christ = anointed; v. 22, Son of man = prophet); Luke 13:33; 24:19; John 3:1,2 (Nicodemus calls Jesus 'Rabbi' and a teacher); John 4:19 (woman at the well perceives him as a prophet); John 6:14; 9:17; 7:40, 41, 52.

All of the other concepts – "only begotten Son of God," "Saviour of the world," "he died for our sins," "was immaculately conceived and born of a virgin," "ascended into heaven," "the second coming of Christ," etc., etc., - came into being several years after Jesus had left this earthly existence.

Remember, Jesus said, as recorded in John 6:6: "It is the spirit that quickeneth; the flesh profiteth nothing [his flesh, your flesh, my flesh, any flesh]: the words that I speak unto you, they are spirit and they are life."

In summary, four principal sources are mainly responsible for the concept of the divinity, yea, the deification of Jesus, and they are: 1. Certain passages within the four Gospels (which were compiled and canonized by the Greeks, the Romans and the Catholic Church); 2. the Epistles of Apostle

Paul; 3. the Catholic Church, and 4. the Nicene Council headed by Constantine the Great, Emperor of Rome.

The deceptions promulgated for centuries by the foregoing sources have been spiritually devastating for million around the globe, resulting in the lack of knowledge of the True God. Jesus, in harmony with the prophets before him, taught mankind thusly: "Thou shalt worship the LORD thy God, and Him only shalt thou serve."

Truly, the impact of Paulineism, Catholicism, and Greco-Romanism has especially effected the thinking of hundreds of millions of people of African ancestry all over the world, and has made it quite difficult for those who strive to keep the way of the ancient biblical prophets alive to increase their ranks. Howbeit, the people of the holy calling will not despair, realizing that the Scriptures – the prophecies of Moses, Isaiah, Daniel, Jesus and the other prophets – cannot be broken. These and other prophecies will be expounded upon in various other topics included in this work.

We have the assurance that through faith in the Most High, righteous living, proper study and continual self-improvement, it shall come to pass in due time that men will one day proclaim anew the words of the prophet Zechariah: ". . . We will go with you, for we have heard that God is with you."

Chapter 3

THE SEVENTH DAY OF THE WEEK
(Commonly Called Saturday)
IS THE MOST HIGH'S HOLY DAY

THE SCRIPTURES TEACH that we must cease from all our work, refrain from all our pleasures, and especially honor the Creator on this, His Holy Day.

The Sabbath is in memory of God's great Creative Work – the heavens, the earth, the seas, and all that is therein, even the entire universe. The Almighty, therefore, commands all mankind to pause in respect to Him and His Creation.

Everything that we have ever seen, heard, tasted, smelled and felt is a part of what The Creator made "in the beginning" (Gen. chapter 1). The Creation is the greatest of all His works – nothing shall ever supersede it! When one pauses on the Sabbath (Saturday), he honors his Creator and at the same time celebrates His Creation.

Say not, "It is the Jewish Sabbath, therefore I am not duty-bound to keep it." The Sabbath was instituted long before there was ever a Jew on earth. For if the Sabbath commandment is "Jewish," then "Thou shalt not steal" and "Thou shalt not kill," etc., would also have to be "Jewish." Nowhere in the Scripture is it referred to as "the Jewish Sabbath," but as "the Sabbath of the LORD thy God."

The original Sabbath of the Bible was changed to Sunday by the Catholic Church in 321 C.E. (A.D.), and then signed into law in the year 325 by Constantine, Emperor of Rome. It was punishable by death if anyone was found observing Saturday (the Sabbath) as a day of rest. Over a period of hundreds of years, millions were put to death at Rome, in Palestine and throughout many parts of the then known world for violating the decree of the Emperor, who himself professed Christianity, thus giving the Church more power to carry out her aim of world domination in both spiritual and secular matters. This was the first combination of Church and State. And "the whole world is now wondering after the Beast" (the Roman Catholic Church), as is stated in a prophecy of Revelation.

1582	OCTOBER				1582	
SUN	MON	TUE	WED	THU.	FRI	SAT
	1	2	3	4	15	16
17	18	19	20	21	22	23
24	25	26	27	28	29	30
31						

When the julian calendar was corrected by Pope Gregory in 1582, ten days were dropped from the calendar count, as it shows here. What would have been Friday the 5th became Friday the 15th. The continuity of the days of the week was not altered or interrupted, nor has it been in _any_ calendar change.

THE UNIVERSAL WEEK

The Language	The Week	The First Day (Sunday)	The Second Day (Monday)	The Third Day (Tuesday)	The Fourth Day (Wednesday)	The Fifth Day (Thursday)	The Sixth Day (Friday)	The Seventh Day (Saturday)
99. Wandak Central Africa	harruye	hde The One	letenin The Two	telago Three	larnba The Fourth	lamien The Fifth	zumma Assembly	aibda Sabbath 64
100. Bagrimma Central Africa	dzamora Collection	lahadi The One	letnin The Two	dzatalati Three	larnba The Fourth	'amisi The Fifth	tdrimma T~e Assembly	sibbedi Sabbath 65
101. Maba Central Africa	mindri Seven	ahad One	ettenin The Two	ettlet The Three	araba Fourth	xamis Fifth	drumma Assembly	sab Sabbath 66
102. MISCELLANEOUS Norman French (10 and 11th Centuries)	Sepmayn. Sepmane	Diemane	Luner	Jeusday, Jeusdye, Jurisdie	Merkedy, Mercuredi, Merdie, Meskerdy	Jeodi	Venerdy, Venerdy, and venedi	Sabbedi, Samadax, Semadi, Sabbath Day 67
103. Ancient French (12 and 13th Centuries)	Semaine, Semeigne		Lundi	Mardi	Merquedi	Joedi, Jeusidi	Vendredi, Vendredi	Samedi, i.e. Sabbath Day 68

The above table is set from "A Chart of the Week," prepared by the Rev. Wm. M. Jones, D. D., a noted antiquarian of London, England, who died a few years ago. This chart is seven feet two inches long and 18½ inches wide. Great research, indefatigable labor, and large expense entered into its preparation. It shows the *unchanged order* of the days of the week among 160 ancient and modern languages and dialects. It gives in nine columns (1) the name of the language, where spoken and used; (2) the name of the week, or the cluster or cycle of seven days; (3-9) the name of each of the days in the original translated or transliterated into English. One hundred eight of these languages show the seventh day of the week to be a holy day. We had no type in which to set some of the most ancient Asiatic languages. Learned missionaries aided in this great work. The testimonies from some of the Asiatic tongues are mere sign characters. The witness to the day of the Sabbath is conclusive. The numbers at the ends are as they are given on the chart. We have omitted from the letters the marks of accent.

31

Chapter 4

IS THE BLACK RACE
THE "CURSE OF HAM"?

HAVE YOU EVER HEARD IT SAID that the Black Race is the "curse of Ham"? If so, do you believe it? If you believe it and are a person of African extraction, how does it make you feel to hear it from pulpit and pew, to be taught it in a Bible college, or to read it in a book?

Those who have promoted this lie over the centuries have used the Bible as their source, just as they have used the Bible to try to justify the nearly 400 years of slavery in the Western Hemisphere.

In the event the reader is not familiar with the biblical narrative, some space will be devoted to the telling of the story.

In the ninth chapter of Genesis is recorded the account of how Noah, after the Flood, planted a vineyard, drank the wine therefrom, became drunk, and was uncovered within his tent (9:21). Noah's son Ham, saw the nakedness of his father, left his tent and told his two brothers of the incident.

When Noah awake from his wine and realized what his son Ham had done to him, Noah cursed Ham's son, Canaan, rather than Han (vs. 24, 25).

Let us now try to bring some semblance of understanding to this very complex and confusing passage.

One Bible commentary attempts to partially excuse Noah's drunkenness by saying that he did not know what the consequences of the excessive drinking of wine would be, since he was the first recorded to plant a vineyard. Nevertheless, the fact remains that Noah became drunk, which resulted in his indecent exposure. If it is true that his son Ham saw his father's nakedness, what is so sinful about one man looking upon another man who is naked? Or does the phrase, *"And Ham saw the nakedness of his father"* (v. 22), have an altogether different meaning other than *"Ham looked upon his father while he was naked"*?

If we invoke the rule, "let scripture explain scripture," and consider the command of the Almighty in Leviticus 18:8, may it not then be proper to conclude that it was not Ham's father that he looked upon, but it was actually his mother? The mandate in Leviticus reads, *"The nakedness of thy fa-ther's wife thou shalt not uncover: **it is thy father's nakedness?***" According to this scripture, a man's nakedness is his wife.

If Ham committed the act, why didn't Noah curse him? Out of Ham's four sons – Cush, Mizraim, Phut, and Canaan – why was Canaan alone cursed? Did Noah experience an after-effect of his inebriation (known in street vernacular as a "hangover"), thus causing him to err in choice and judgment? An admonition which appears much later in scripture reads: "It is not for kings, O Lemuel, it is not for kings to drink wine, nor for princes strong drink: lest they drink, and forget the law, and pervert the judgment of any of the afflicted" (Prov. 31:4, 5).

One may rebut: "Did not God say that He would visit the iniquity of the fathers upon the children . . ."? Yes, He did; but He added, ". . . unto the third and fourth generations of them that hate Me . . ." (Exodus 20:5). There exists no record of Ham or Canaan as haters of God. Furthermore, we refuse to believe that any human being has the power to curse a man and all his descendants for ever and ever. Only the Divine Being could do that.

The supposed curse placed upon Canaan for Ham's folly was more severe than the curse pronounced upon Cain, who murdered his brother, righteous Abel. It was God Himself who sentenced Cain, yet there was not included any punishment whatsoever upon his seed after him (Genesis 4:8-15).

(Please pardon the following parenthetical digression. But speaking of Cain, more than 65 years ago while attending grade school in Philadelphia, this author had in his possession a public school textbook which carried within its pages an awfully horrendous statement on the origin of the Black race. The writer of that book (the name of whom and the title of which we do not recall) undoubtedly had read in Genesis that "God set a mark upon Cain, lest any finding him should kill him." The writer's interpretation of that passage was so heart-rending that we still remember it verbatim to this day: The "mark" set upon Cain was described by her as follows:

("It is believed that the mark which the Lord set upon Cain was that He turned him black, and this was the beginning of the Black race." How absurd, how ridiculous! So much so that we refuse to dignify such a commentary with a response. The author of this book has known since the age of seven that the prophets, priests, kings and nations of Old Testament times were all of the Black race.)

The Canaanites, descended from Canaan, represented only one segment of the many branches of the Black race during that era, yet those who subscribe to this "Curse of Ham" nonsensical hypothesis would have you believe that every Black person who has ever lived, who is living now, and who ever will live was cursed from the moment of Noah's utterance until time is no more. And the saddest commentary of all is that millions of people of African descent believe the "hype."

Combined, more than 32 nations descended from Ham and Canaan. So powerful were the Canaanites that after the death of Noah they enjoyed more than 1,000 years of prosperity, and could not be entirely driven out of their land by the Israelites during Joshua's conquest of Canaan, but dwelt with the Israelites for many centuries thereafter

The patriarch Abraham, among the most faithful and righteous men of recorded history, is very much an integral part of this discussion. Born in Ur of the Chaldees (also known as Babylonia), a place inhabited by the descendants of Ham, the story of Abraham is well known in Judaic, Christian and Islamic circles, and research reveals that he is the only person in the entire Bible whom God called "My friend." This utterance appears in Isaiah 41:8, nearly 1,100 years after his death. The Book of Chronicles and the Epistle of James also mention Abrahan as God's friend.

At birth he was named *Abram* – the Hebrew transliteration of which is AV-RAM – meaning "exalted father." One hundred years later his named was changed to Abraham – AV-RAHAM – "father of multitudes" – "for a father of a multitude of nations have I made you . . ." (The last reference in quotations is from the Hebrew Scriptures.) The final three letters of Abraham are 'h-a-m' – "HAM." Would the Almighty in blessing "His friend" name him after a cursed person?

Definition of "Ham," and His Descendants' Contributions

Ham (*dark, sunburnt*). One of the sons of Noah, perhaps the third. Settled in Africa (Ps. 78:51, 105:23, 106:22), and also sent many branches into Asia (Canaanites). There is no ancient name so well preserved and located. Ham is identified with JUPITER AMMON, and also ZEUS (Greek gods), because both words are derived from a root meaning hot, fervent, or sunburnt. The descendants of Ham – Egypt and Babylon – led the way as pioneers in art, literature and science. Mankind at the present day lies under infinite obligations to the genius and industry of those early ages, more especially for alphabetic writing, weaving, cloth, architecture, astronomy, plastid art, sculpture, navigation and agriculture. The art of instruments is also represented, and music indirectly, by drawings of instruments. (From Smith's Bible Dictionary of 1871.)

Considering the wisdom and indispensable contributions to civilization of the ancient Hamitic race cited in all of the aforementioned, certainly these could not be the marks of a cursed people! Abraham was one of them, and he is "God's friend for ever) II Chron. 20:7).

THE SONS AND GRANDSONS OF HAM, AND THEIR LOCATION.

CUSH	Seba,	Meroe, in Egypt.
	Havilah,	Abyssinia.
	Sabtah,	S. W. coast Red Sea.
	Raamah, { Sheba, Dedan. }	Arabia, Persia.
	Sabtechah,	Ethiopia.
	Nimrod (Belus),	Shinar. Chaldæa.
MIZRAIM	Ludim,	West, in Africa.
	Anamim,	Mareotis.
	Lehabim,	Libyans.
	Naphtuhim,	Memphis.
	Pathrusim,	Thebes. Pathros.
	Casluhim,	Arabia Petræa.
	Caphtorim,	Damietta.
PHUT	Phut,	Lybians.
CANAAN	Sidon,	Sidon and Tyre.
	Heth,	Hittites.
	Jebusites,	Jerusalem.
	Amorites,	Judæa.
	Girgasite,	Gergesenes.
	Hivite,	Shechem.
	Arkite,	Arke.
	Sinite,	Sinnas.
	Arvadite,	Island of Arvad.
	Zemarite,	Sumrah (ruin).
	Hamathite,	Hamath.

(HAM)

"You can easily forgive a child

for being afraid of the dark,

but the real tragedy comes

when men are afraid of the light!"

Chapter 5

The Prophecies of Moses in Deuteronomy 28 and Jesus in Luke 21 Foretell the African Slave Trade and Slavery in the Western Hemisphere

These Prophecies Could Not Possibly Apply To Any Other People on Earth, Except the Enslaved Africans and Their Descendants

"AND THE LORD SHALL SCATTER THEE among all peoples, from the one end of the earth even unto the other end of the earth; and there thou shalt serve other gods, which thou hast not known, nor thy fathers, even wood and stone. And the LORD shall bring thee back into Egypt in ships, by the way whereof I said unto thee: Thou shalt see it no more again; and there ye shall sell yourselves unto your enemies for bondmen and for bondwomen, and no man shall buy you" (Deut. 28:64, 68).

(The Hebrew Holy Scriptures, English Translation)

"AND WHEN YE SHALL SEE JERUSALEM compassed with armies, then know that the desolation thereof is nigh. Then let them which are in Judæa flee to the mountains; and let them which are in the midst of it depart out; and let not them that are in the countries enter thereinto. For these be the days of vengeance, that all things which are written may be fulfilled . . . For there shall be great distress in the land, and wrath upon this people. And they shall fall by the edge of the sword, and shall be led away captive into all nations; and Jerusalem shall be trodden down of the Gentiles, until the times of the Gentiles be fulfilled" (Luke 21:20-24, KJV).

THE 28TH CHAPTER OF DEUTERONOMY is one of the most astounding chapters in the entire Bible, for it outlines – more
than any other passage – step by step in explicit detail the
blessings which would come upon the Israelites and overtake
them if they would hearken to and obey the commandments of
their God (verses 1-14), and the curses which would befall
them if they failed to hearken and obey (verses 15-68).

Moses, Israel's foremost prophet, through Divine Revelation, set before the people the all-important "If-Then" factor:
"And it shall come to pass, IF thou wilt hearken diligently
unto the voice of the LORD thy God, to observe and to do all
His commandments which I command thee this day, THEN
the LORD thy God shall set thee on high above all nations of
the earth . . ." The "If-Then" factor is applied again, as
pertains to the curses, in verse 15-68: "But it shall come to
pass, IF thou wilt not hearken unto the voice of the LORD thy
God, to observe to do all His commandments and His statutes
which I command thee this day; THEN all these curses shall
come upon thee, and overtake thee . . ."

Throughout the history of the Hebrew Israelite people,
especially from Moses downward, when they obeyed the
Creator they enjoyed an abundance of prosperity, and even
during the time of war they were victorious. But when they
became estranged from the Almighty, calamity and peril followed.

The thinking is very widespread among many today that
the Israelite Way of Life (which in modern day has come to be
called by some, "Judaism") is only for people of a certain
race or nationality. According to the teaching and example of
Moses and the prophets, however, this is not true; for beside
the 600,000 Israelite men – not including children – who
marched out of Egypt during the Exodus, there was also *a*

mixed multitude of non-Israelites accompanying them (Ex. 12:38). Egypt, remember, had amassed great wealth and splendor, had become the greatest of all the nations, and had living within her borders immigrants from many other countries. After Israel's departure from Egypt the mixed multitude was assimilated into the Israelite nation, and they, too, embraced the commandments, statutes and judgments taught by Moses. (The term "mixed multitude" is defined as, *a great mixture; a medley of people.)*

Israel was thrust into many a captivity during biblical times because of her disobedience to God, but He always gave her a gracious Return. Prophecy, like history, often repeats itself. **What is so amazing about the 28th chapter of Deuteronomy is that in its enumeration of the curses** (vss. 15-68), **it not only foretells what will befall the descendants of the Original Israelites (who were a nation of Black people), but this prophecy stretches its long arm through 32 centuries, touching today almost the whole of the Black race globally.**

There is a plan in place and at work among many leading religionists worldwide to systematically keep our people in the back of the Bible so that they will never know who they are. Deuteronomy 28 gives us a perfect description of what has happened to us as a race, portrays our present-day dilemma – as though it were written yesterday – and is entirely too striking to be coincidental.

Of the 54 verses which comprise the curses, we find 31 of them to be of the utmost importance for review. Highlighted will be the following: Verses 16-18, 20, 25, 28-34, 36, 37, 41, 43, 44-50, 53, 58, 59, 64-68. Commentary will follow where necessary.

16. "Cursed shalt thou be in the city, and cursed shalt thou be in the field.

> 17. Cursed shall be thy basket and thy store. 18. Cursed shall be the fruit of thy body, and the fruit of thy land, and the increase of thy kine, and the flocks of thy sheep. 20. The LORD shall send upon thee cursings, vexation, and rebuke, in all that thou settest thine hand unto for to do until thou be destroyed, and until thou perish quickly, because of the wickedness of thy doings, whereby thou hast forsaken Me. 25. The LORD shall cause thee to be smitten before thine enemies: thou shalt go out one way against them, and flee seven ways before them: <u>and shalt be removed into all the kingdoms of the earth.</u>"

Certainly our enemies through the centuries have smitten us beyond measure. We have been removed far and wide from our homelands of both Jerusalem and Africa.

> 29-33. "And thou shalt grope at noonday, as the blind gropeth in darkness. and thou shalt not prosper in thy ways: and shalt be only oppressed and spoiled evermore, and no man shall save thee. Thou shalt betroth a wife, and another man shall lie with her; thou shalt build a house, and thou shalt not dwell therein; thou shalt plant a vineyard, and shalt not gather the grapes thereof. Thine ox shall be slain before thine eyes, and thou shalt not eat thereof; thine ass shall be violently taken away from before thy face, and shall not be restored to thee; thy sheep shall be given unto thine enemies, and thou shalt have none to rescue them. Thy sons and thy daughters shall be given unto another people, and thine eyes shall look, and fail with longing for them all the day long: and there shall be no might in thine hand. The fruit of thy land, and all thy labours, shall a nation which thou knewest not eat up, and thou shalt be only oppressed and crushed alway."

We have experienced an ongoing lack of prosperity as a people; constantly oppressed, no one has come to our rescue. The slavemaster laid with our mothers, wives, sisters and daughters; land and cattle have been taken away, especially in the south, even during post-slavery years. As we helplessly looked on, our sons and daughters were sold to another people. Nations whom we knew not went into western and southern Africa and possessed all their natural resources and wildlife.

> 36, 37. "The LORD shall bring thee, and thy king which thou hast set over thee, unto a nation which neither thou nor thy fathers have known: and there shalt thou serve other gods, wood and stone. And thou shalt become an astonishment, a proverb, and a byword, among all nations whither the LORD shall lead thee."

Kings, queens, princes and princesses were brought to various nations which our fathers had never before known. There we were introduced to and forced to serve a different god from "THE GREAT ONE" known to the Africans. We were made to worship under the sign of the Cross, often made of wood and stone. The Black race is the most hated race on the face of the earth.

> 41, 43, 44. "Thou shalt beget sons and daughters, but thou shalt not enjoy them; for they shall go into captivity. The stranger that is within thee shall get up above thee very high, and thou shalt come down very low. He shall lend to thee, and thou shalt not lend to him.: and he shall be the head, and thou shalt be the tail."

Europeans and Asisns come to this country and get ahead in a very short time, opening businesses and receiving great recognition. We as a people are still at the bottom of the barrel and "are the tail."

> 48-50. "Therefore thou shalt serve thine enemies which the LORD shall send against thee, in hunger, and in nakedness, and in want of all things: and he shall put a yoke of iron upon thy neck, until he have destroyed thee. The LORD shall bring a nation against thee from far, from the end of the earth, as swift as the eagle flieth; a nation whose tongue thou shalt not understand: a nation of fierce countenance, which shall not regard the person of the old, nor show favor to the young."

Our foreparents worked the fields in hunger, thirst and near-nakedness – just a piece of cloth around their loins – and were treated worse than animals. ". . . As swift as the eagle flieth" (vs. 49): the symbol of the United States is the eagle; their countenance was fierce, and we did not understand their tongue (language). They had no mercy on the old or the young.

> 58, 59. "If thou wilt not observe to do all the words of this law that are written in this book, that thou mayest fear this glorious and fearful name, THE LORD THY GOD; then the LORD will make thy plagues wonderful, and the plagues of thy seed, even great plagues, and of long continuance, and sore sicknesses, and of long continuance."

To be a whole person one must keep the Law of God and have a reverence and respect for this fearful and glorious name, THE LORD THY GOD – not the name of Abraham, Moses, Isaiah, Jeremiah, or Jesus, but this fearful and glorious name, THE LORD THY GOD. All the biblical prophets, including Jesus, taught reverence for the Name of God.

> 64-68. "And the LORD shall scatter thee among all people, from the one end of the earth even unto the other; and there thou shalt serve other

gods, which neither thou nor thy fathers have known, even wood and stone. And among those nations shalt thou find no ease, neither shall the sole of thy feet have rest: but the LORD shall give thee there a trembling heart, and failing of eyes, and sorrow of mind. And thy life shall hang in doubt before thee; and thou shalt fear day and night, and shalt have none assurance of thy life. In the morning thou shalt say, Would to God it were evening! And at evening thou shalt say, Would to God it were morning! for the fear of thine heart wherewith thou shalt fear, and for the sight of thine eyes which thou shalt see. And the LORD shall bring thee into Egypt again with ships, by the way whereof I spake unto thee, Thou shalt see it no more again; and there ye shall sell yourselves unto your enemies for bondmen and bondwomen, and no man shall buy you."

Our race is in great trouble and distress; we find no ease wherever we go. Only the Most High can bring about our redemption and salvation. The prophecy says that we would come into Egypt again by *ships:* the Western Hemisphere mostly where we were scattered is "the second Egypt," and we arrived there by ships. Others bought and sold us, and we sold each other to our enemies, as prophesied. No man shall intercede on behalf of the people of African ancestry except he is sent by the Almighty Himself to lift our people worldwide out of the horrible pit of degradation. The only way out is through the Eternal One, His commandments and the teaching of His prophets.

Rudolph Yehuda Windsor's two startling books, *From Babylon To Timbuktu* and *The Valley of the Dry Bones;* Ella Hughley's scholarly work, *The Truth About Black Biblical Hebrew Israelites,* and this book, THE DECEIVING OF THE BLACK RACE, are all wake-up calls to men and women all over this world, but to people of the Black race in particular – the disenfranchised, the downtrodden, the outcast – to reclaim the King of the universe, the Eternal One of Abraham, Isaac and Jacob. We implore you to leave the beggarly elements of the camouflaged idolatrous worship, as did Abraham of old (Joshua 24:2), and return to the God of your forefathers. The LORD of Hosts has promised, in the words of His prophets, to abundantly pardon (Isaiah 55:7).

The Prophecy of Yeshua (Jesus) in Luke 21:20-24, and Its Connection with Deuteronomy 28

"AND WHEN YE SHALL SEE JERUSALEM compassed with armies, then know that the desolation thereof is nigh. Then let them which are in Judæa flee to the mountains; and let them that are in the midst of it depart out; and let not them that are in the countries enter there into. For these be the days of vengeance, that all things which are written may be fulfilled. But woe unto them that are with child, and to them that give suck in those days! for there shall be great distress in the land, and wrath upon this people. And they shall fall by the edge of the sword, <u>and shall be led away captive into all nations:</u> and Jerusalem shall be trodden down of the Gentiles, until the times of the Gentiles be fulfilled."

These five simple verses, though not nearly as verbal as the prophecy of Moses in Deuteronomy 28, hold a very important clue as to how thousands of the descendants of the ancient Hebrew Israelites became inhabitants of the New World.

In this passage Yeshua is foretelling the destruction of Jerusalem and what would befall the Israelite people during that siege and destruction.

The year is circa 33 C.E. (A.D.); Rome is already in control of Jerusalem, and it no longer belongs to the Israelites. There is much resentment against Rome by all the religious leaders and their followers – John the Proselytizer, Yeshua (Jesus), the Pharisees, Sadducees, and Zealots.

Rome had invaded Jerusalem and was grinding its heels on the necks of the Black Israelites of Yeshua's time, just as the Dutch did in South Africa centuries ago to the indigenous people there.

Yeshua (Jesus) was simply reinforcing the prophesies of Moses, Daniel and some of the other prophets of Old Testament times when he told of Jerusalem's future downfall.

The Roman-Jewish War, history records, began in 66 C.E. (A.D.), about 33 years after Yeshua's "crucifixion," and lasted for four years. First the Romans compassed the city (Luke 21:20), just as Nebuchadnezzar had done in the days of Jeremiah at Jerusalem's first destruction; then finally, in the year 70 A.D., Titus and the Roman army destroyed Jerusalem, laying the city and the Temple level with the ground.

Yeshua's (Jesus') admonition to the people was, "If you are in Judæa when the Romans strike, flee to the mountains; if you are in Jerusalem hasten to leave it, and if you are outside of the city do not enter into it" (vs. 21). *"For these be the days of vengeance* (vs. 22a): God will once again inflict vengeance upon His people for their disobedience and for the way they have ignored and killed His prophets through the centuries. *"That all things that are written may be fulfilled"* (vs. 22b): All things that are written in the prophecies of Moses and Daniel concerning Israel's scattering and how this mighty world power – the Greco-Roman Empire – would cast the truth to the ground, and would practice and prosper (Daniel 8:9-13; 8:21, Alexander the Great of Greece; 8:24,25).

The Israelites in Jerusalem during this war were in great distress, and the wrath of God was upon them (Luke 21:23). There were many good and righteous people in Jerusalem at that time, however, but both the righteous and the wicked suffered during the crisis. The prophecy of Daniel had to be fulfilled: *"And his* [the Grecian] *power shall be mighty, but not by his own power* [he shall have Rome to help him]; *and he shall destroy wonderfully* [terribly], *and shall prosper, and practice, and shall destroy the mighty and the holy people* (Daniel 8:24). "The mighty and holy people referred to here are the people of Israel who were the holy and righteous ones living in Jerusalem and throughout Judæa during the aforementioned Roman-Jewish War.

Thousands fell by the edge of the sword (Luke 20-24a). Fleeing for their lives, thousands more escaped into various countries of Asia and Africa, thus fulfilling the prophecy, in part: *"And they shall be led away captive into all nations"* (vs. 24b). As a result of that *leading away,* today there are Chinese Jews and Indian Jews who over the centuries have taken on the features of the indigenous people of those countries.

Still running for their lives from the onslaught of the Roman sword, thousands went into Africa, some eventually crossing the Sahara Desert and settling in various countries of the Mother Continent. Many years passed over, and West Africa eventually became the home of not a few of the descendants of the Israelites who were originally driven out of Jerusalem. Wherever they settled they continued their Hebrew customs and traditions. *The Hebrewisms of West Africa* by the late Joseph Williams of Boston College; *The Hebrew Heritage of Black Africa* by Steven Jacobs; *From Babylon To Timbuktu* by Rudolph Windsor, and *The Truth About Black Biblical Hebrew Israelites* by Ella Hughley, all reveal that after the war in 70 C.E., Black Israelites/Jews in the Diaspora have been discovered throughout the length and breadth of Africa.

The Israelites who had lived in West Africa for more than 1,400 years were caught up, along with many other African tribes, in the African Slave Trade of the 14th, 15th, 16th, and 17th centuries. Thus the prophecies of Moses in Deuteronomy 28, and of Yeshua (Jesus) in Luke 21 were fulfilled when the posterity of ancient Israel were led led away captive into rigorous slavery and sold to their enemies as bondmen and bondwomen.

Yeshua's prophecy closes thusly (vs. 24b): *"And Jerusalem shall be trodden down of the Gentiles . . ."* Not only was the city of Jerusalem trodden down by the Romans, but also the people – those who inhabited the city – were trodden down. For how long? *"Until the times of the Gentiles be fulfilled."* This strongly suggests that our degraded condition will not last forever, but only "until the times of the Gentiles be fulfilled." ("Times" in prophecy means "years".)

Just as there has been a mass exodus of the Black race from the True Knowledge of the True God – both ignorantly and willfully – there must now be an overflowing Return to the will of the Almighty if we expect to rise again as a people. Seek, and ye shall find!

SCRIPTURAL CONSIDERATIONS

"And thou shalt love the LORD *thy God with all thine heart, and with all thy soul, and with all thy might."*
(Deuteronomy 6:5; Matthew 22:37)

". . . Thou shalt love thy neighbor as thyself."
(Leviticus 19:18; Matthew 22:39)

"My people are destroyed for the lack of knowledge: because thou hast rejected knowledge, I will also reject thee, that thou shalt be no priest to Me: seeing thou hast forgotten the law of thy God, I will also forget thy children."
(Hosea 4:6)

"Who hath directed the Spirit of the LORD, *or being His counselor hath taught Him? With whom took He counsel, and who instructed Him in the path of judgment, and taught Him knowledge, and showed to Him the way of understanding? To whom then will ye liken God? or what likeness will ye compare unto Him? To whom then will ye liken Me, or shall I be equal? saith the Holy One."*
(Isaiah 40:11, 14, 18, 25)

"Behold, the days come, saith the LORD *God, that I will send a famine in the land, not a famine of bread, nor a thirst for water, but of the hearing of the words of the* LORD: *and they shall wander from sea to sea, and from the north even to the east, they shall run to and fro to seek the word of the* LORD, *and shall not find it."*
(Amos 8:11, 12)

Chapter 6

THERE ARE *"TWO JESUSES"* IN THE NEW TESTAMENT

***The "False Jesus" has been "blown up" in
The New Testament and in church pulpits,
and the "Real Jesus" has been "covered up"!***

AT FIRST GLANCE, this heading could have a tendency to appear very misleading. When the author posted it on a flyer as a lecture topic back in 1987, many began citing those recorded in the Greek Scriptures bearing the name *Jesus*. "O yes," some exclaimed, "there is Jesus Christ, then there is Jesus, called Justus, Paul's disciple at Rome (Col. 4:11). Some even expressed knowledge of a Jesus the son of Sirach, in the Book of Ecclesiasticus of the Apochrapha. The point, however, was entirely missed; the extent and intent of the heading go much deeper than it appears.

The first, or real, Jesus – the historical Jesus of Nazareth – was a human being. The second, or false, Jesus, whom to many is a Man-God – is a creation of the Greeks, the Romans, and the Roman Catholic Church. The real Jesus was not a Christian, was not the founder of Christianity, and did not bring a new revelation to mankind.

Yeshua ben Yosef, whom the Greeks called *Iesous Christos* (Jesus Christ), was a prophet of God; no more, no less. He was born in a natural way – through a biological father and mother. He grew as a child, he ate, slept, cried, became angry, hungered, bled and died, as do all other humans.

49

This highly spiritual being, this man of the cosmos, this man whom the people of his day heralded time after time as 'Rabbi' and 'Teacher' (John 3:1, 2); 'holy one of God' (Mark 1:24); 'son of David' (through lineage, Mark 10:46); 'Prophet' (John 4:19), etc., never intended or attempted to portray himself as supernatural or to exalt himself as an equal to the Almighty. The masses are caught up with what the wicked powers of those times have said about Yeshua years after his death rather than whom he proclaimed himself to be, or how the people who walked and talked with him perceived him.

Whoso Readeth Let him Understand

When Yeshua called himself the son of God, he did so with explanation. The grandest and clearest example of this is recorded in John 10:30-36. This passage, when read and properly understood, dispels all arguments in favor of what has been established by the evil triune power for nearly 2,000 years: That Jesus was God become man, the Deity incarnate, immaculately conceived by the Holy Ghost, and given birth by a woman who had never been and never was to be intimately touched by a man. (See chapter on *Why Jesus Called Himself the Son of God.*) These concepts and hundreds more are all hold-overs from Egyptian and Babylonian Mythology, and were easily and readily adopted by the Greeks and Romans as a part of their mythology during their more than 700-year world rule (circa 323 B.C.-430 A.D.), (The mythology of the virgin birth of Jesus will be discussed in depth in the chapter entitled *Alleged Christological References In Scripture,* where it will be conclusively proved that Isaiah 7:14 has absolutely nothing to do with the Immaculate Conception or Jesus' birth.) Remember, Alexander the Great of Greece conquered the then known world 300 years before Christ. Greece under Alexander invaded and captured the Black African country of Egypt, stealing all her 4,000 years of wisdom and claiming it as her (Greece's) own. Today, through centuries of sword-wielding, lies and deceit, Greece is known as the Cradle of Civilization.

New Testament Flavored with Greek, Roman and Catholic Church Influence

The Greek, Roman, and Catholic Church influence in the New Testament has created a Jesus whom Jesus would never recognize were he on earth today. It was the Greeks who took away his beautiful Hebrew name, Yeshua ben Yosef (Joshua son of Joseph), and replaced it with Jesus (the second syllable of which borders on the Greek god Zeus). When Jesus lived no one knew him as *Jesus Christ!* Were he across the street right now, and you shouted out to him, "JESUS!" or "JESUS CHRIST!", he wouldn't even respond. In other words, Jesus never heard the name *Jesus* nor the title *Christ.* He spoke two languages, Hebrew and Aramaic; he did not speak Greek. Furthermore, the title *Saint,* which appears before the names of Matthew, Mark, Luke, and John (the supposed writers of the Gospels), was placed there by the Catholic Church.

We have mentioned earlier how that Yeshua referred to himself, in a few instances in the Gospels, as the Son of God. But more noteworthy is the fact that in more than eighty instances he declares that he is the *Son of man!* Throughout the Book of Ezekiel God addresses that prophet as *Son of man."* Additionally, in Exodus 4:22 the Most High calls Israel His son; in II Samuel 7:13 and I Chronicles 17:11-13 He calls Solomon His son, and in Isaiah 43:6, the dispersed, outcast and downtrodden of Israel are rendered as the sons and daughters of God. Yes, God was Yeshua's father; but he taught that God is also your Father, saying, "When you pray, say, 'Our Father . . .'" (Matt. 6:9). We also agree that Yeshua was God's son, and if you live a life of righteousness and sincerity, as did he, you, too, will be a son or a daughter of God.

Yeshua was consistent in his teaching, and place after place he gave credence to Moses and the prophets. As painful as it is, the truth must be told: There are many expressions in the New Testament, although they appear in red (that is, in a Red-Letter Edition), that Yeshua did not say, but were placed there for the purpose of deceiving the world and creating a false Jesus. As a case in point, and to coincide with the topic under discussion, let us consider the passage found in John 3:18: "He that believeth on him is not condemned: but he that believeth not is condemned already, because he hath not believed in the name of the only begotten Son of God." These words are attributed to Yeshua, but they are inconsistent with what is contained in the Scriptures which he so devotedly embraced, and therefore we have difficulty believing that the quotation is actually his. Throughout the Old Testament, only the name of The Almighty is exalted and holy, and it is hard to conceive that Yeshua would in any way place himself in competition with the Most High. To condemn all who do not believe in his name – "in the name of the only begotten Son of God" – is a very far-reaching indictment. It would have been more acceptable had the condemnation been inflicted upon all those who rejected his prophetship, his words and his works (Matt. 13:57, 58; John 6:63 and 13:11), but not for refusing to believe in Yeshua's name.

Here is just one example of many of what those who compiled and canonized the New Testament did in their effort to force a prophecy from the Old Testament to fit the New: In Psalm 2:7 they extracted the words which God had said to

David, king of Israel, took them out of context, and applied them to Yeshua. Psalm 2:7 reads as follows:

"I [David] will declare the decree: The LORD has said unto me [David], Thou art my beloved Son, this day have I begotten thee." (In the Hebrew Holy Scriptures, English translation, the word My is capitalized – as it is a pronoun in this case for "LORD"; and the word son is with a small s.)

The New Testament contains an abundance of beauty, truth and wisdom, but the ruling powers of those times have distorted and falsified the utterances and writings of some of the Greek Scripture's central figures. The Catholic Church has said in one of its historical statements back in the fourth century: "The Church made the Bible [New Testament], the Bible did not make the Church."

We must conclude, therefore, that all things whatsoever recorded in the New Testament which are contradictory to or inconsistent with the teaching of Moses and the Prophets should not be considered as spoken through Divine Revelation or Inspiration. An instance, among hundreds, is John chapter 1, where "the Word" (Jesus) is said to have been in beginning with God, and "the_Word" (Jesus) was God, and then it states that "the world was made by him" (Jesus). How blasphemous! This chapter could not possibly have been written by the disciple John, but is an insertion by the Greeks, the Romans and the Catholic Church, who compiled and canonized the New Testament, in their zeal to make Jesus God.

"Idol" and "Idolatry" Defined

Smith's Bible Dictionary defines an *idol* as "An image or anything used as an object of worship in place of the true God." *Idolatry* is defined as: "Strictly speaking, denotes the worship of deity in a visible form, whether the images to which homage is paid are symbolical representations of the true God or of the false divinities which have been made the objects of worship in His stead."

Those who pray to Jesus or worship him or any other being or object other than the True and Living Most High God, are engaging in idolatry. Jesus and the prophets before him taught thusly: ". . . They that worship God must worship Him in spirit and in truth"; and, "Thou shalt worship *the Lord thy God, and Him only shalt thou serve."*

How wonderful it would be if those of the Christian persuasion would engage themselves more in *"Jesus-ology"* rather than in *"Jesus-olatry"* – that is, in the study of Jesus, rather than in the worship of Jesus.

The Future Evaluation of Jesus

Charles Potter, in his book entitled *The Story of Religion* sums up his chapter on *JESUS* in this way:

"The next great 'Life of Jesus' will forever dispose of the myth that the Man of Galilee was a god who came down to earth, a deity incarnate, bringing an absolutely new revelation to mankind.

"Jesus will be seen by men of tomorrow as a student of his national literature, possessed of its quaint superstitions and all its lore, but possessed of its treasures as well. He will be known to have made few original additions to the ethics of his countrymen, but to have been so steeped in the literature of his own godly people that he remolded it into mosaics of sermons and explanatory parables so artistically and ethically beautiful that they will last as long as the race of men endures. Even more than that, he will be thought of, by Jew and Gentile of tomorrow, as a man who really lived the best truth he knew, who took what he had read and thought and interpreted it to humanity by embodying it in his own life.

"He successfully demonstrated truth by incarnating right-eousness. When men hereafter bow to him, it will not be in homage to a deity, but in recognition of a superior craftsman in the art of living.".

Chapter 7

WHY JESUS CALLED HIMSELF "THE SON OF GOD"

SOME HISTORIANS place Yeshua as having once belonged to a small Jewish sect known as the Essenes, while others totally disagree. But whether he did or not, when you consider the morality, ethics and customs practiced by this band of God-fearing men who settled in the isolated areas of the Judæan desert and in the vicinity of the Dead Sea, it stands to reason that Jesus must have been very much aware of the existence of this pious order, as his life in so many ways parallels that of the Essenes.

THE ESSENES possessed a spiritual knowledge of the Divine Law, and arose about 200 B.C. Their chief city was Engedi. The name is supposed to mean *silent, mysterious* or *pious*. The origin of the party was rather in a certain tendency of religious thought among all classes towards an ideal purity and divine communion.

Next to God, Moses was honored, the Sabbath was carefully kept; food was eaten only when prepared by their own members, and never cooked on the Sabbath; and they practiced self-denial, temperance, and agriculture. Slavery, war and commerce were forbidden. They were very regular in their devotions; before sunrise they began their prayer and praise, and grace before and after meals; ate from one kind of food at a meal; disallowed oaths, holding truth to be sacred; held all things in common. Their system was a compound of mystical and ceremonial elements. The applicant for membership was obliged to live a year outside the order, but keeping its rules, having received as badge an ax, a white apron and a white dress. One year he would share in the ablutions but not in the meals. After two more years he was admitted to full membership, solemnly binding himself to piety to God, justice to men, to hate the wicked, assist the righteous, injure no one, speak the truth, avoid robbery and theft, and keep the rules and secrets of the society. Some of their rules were: To bathe if touched by a stranger, or a lower grade of their own order, and before and after meals, and other natural acts; not to spit in an assembly, and if so not on the right side; the social meal was a sacrament. Baptisms produced bodily purity, which led to 2, celibacy, and 3. spiritual purity, and 4, to a meek and lowly spirit, banishing all anger and malice, thus reaching 5, holiness, and could prophesy, and advancing to 7, could perform miraculous cures, raising the dead, attaining finally to the lofty state of Elijah, the forerunner of the Messiah.

Jesus alludes to the Essenes in Matt. 5:34, "swear not at all," and in Matt. 19:12, "who abstain from marriage for the kingdom of heaven's sake."

The Essenes disappeared after Jerusalem's destruction in 70 A.D.

Addressing God as "Father" was not new to the times of Yeshua (Jesus), as the people of his age were well versed in the ancient Holy Scriptures passed down by their Hebrew progenitors. In fact, the sacred Scriptures they had in their possession were what is erroneously called "the Old Testament" and the Apocrypha, as well as other books of Hebrew literature, which included Jasher, I and II Enoch, and the Testament of the Twelve Patriarchs. The latter three were best sellers during the time of Yeshua. What is referred to as "the New Testament" was not to be completed in its final state until the fourth century C.E. (A.D.).

Yeshua and the people of his time who worshipped the True and Living God had vehemently searched the Torah, the Psalms, the Prophets and other sacred literature, and were familiar with such passages as "Is not He [the LORD] thy father that hath made thee?" (Deut. 32:6); "A Father to the fatherless is God" (Psa. 68:5); "I [God] am a father to Israel (Jer. 31:9); "Thou art our father . . ." (Isa. 63:16), and others.

When one considers the high spiritual plain on which Yeshua lived, and couple that with his many acts of humanitarianism to the spiritually, mentally, morally and physically dejected, one should be able to clearly see how easy it was for him to say, "God is my Father," and "I am God's son."

Within the tenth chapter of John, verses 30-36, lies the answer to the subject at hand, "Why Jesus Called Himself the Son of God." Let us now walk slowly through each of the six verses in question, and see if we can put the matter to rest, once and for all.

John 10:10 (Yeshua speaking): "I and my Father are one."

INTERPRETATION: Yeshua is by no means implying here that God and he are the same being, but rather, that there is a oneness that exists between the two of them. Anyone who is in complete harmony with the Most High's Creation, His Laws and His Prophets, surely it can be said of him that "God and he are one." Moses and God were one; for Moses put up no opposition even when told by the Almighty, "You shall not go over into the Promised Land." All true prophets of God and true children of God exemplify a harmonious balance between Creator and creature which establishes an inexplainable bond of unity; thus they are one with the Almighty.

John 10:31: "Then the Jews took up stones to stone him."

INTERPRETATION: This is a very unfair and unjust rendering, as it strongly infers that all Jews participated in Yeshua's would-be stoning. It would have been better to have used the phrase *"then some of the Jews, . . ."* and not just *"the Jews."* Yeshua's disciples were Jews; we are sure that they were not among the stone-gatherers. This is why the writer, in vs. 31, all the more should have qualified the phrase *"the Jews."* Every leader of people has both friends and enemies among his own race and religion – those who believe and those who do not; and so it was with Yeshua. In many instances the Jews of Yeshua's day were intentionally portrayed like the Black race in our day is portrayed – as the villain. However, there were those among his countrymen who did receive him and his message. (See John 8:31, 32.) Lastly, those who took up the stones to stone Yeshua did so because they misunderstood his sayings. Many did not understand his message then, and hundreds of millions more today yet do not.

Verse 33: "The Jews answered him, saying, 'For a good work we stone thee not; but for blasphemy; and because that thou, being a man, maketh thyself God.'"

INTERPRETATION: Yeshua's accusers charged him with blasphemy; he was speaking spiritually, but they were listening carnally. They took *"I and my Father are one"* (vs. 30) to mean that "I [Yeshua] am God, and God is me." On another occasion the disciple Philip said to Yeshua, "Show us the Father . . ." (John 14:8). Yeshua answered him (vs. 9), "He that hath seen me hath seen the Father . . ." When men and women walk with God, as did Enoch and Noah of old, people will behold them and will see God – in them. Yeshua so lived that when men saw him, they saw God in him, and he taught others to do likewise. (See Matt. 5:16.)

Verses 34-36: "Yeshua answered them, Is it not written in your law, 'I said, Ye are gods?' If He called them gods, unto whom the word of God came, and the scripture cannot be broken,: Say ye of him, whom the Father hath sanctified, and sent into the world, 'Thou blasphemeth'; because I said, I am the Son of God?"

INTERPRETATION: "Is it not written in your law, 'I said, Ye are gods?'" Here, Yeshua is reminding them of what is recorded in the Scriptures that they say they believe in – "your law" – Psalm 82:6, where it says, "I [God] have said, Ye are gods" (small *g*). He continues, "If He [God] called them gods, unto whom the word of God came [or to whom the word of god was revealed], and the scripture cannot be broken [that which has been foretold in scripture by the righteous cannot fail]; (vs. 36) "Say ye [his enemies] of me [Yeshua], whom the Father has sanctified [set apart, as God did Jeremiah (1.5) and all the other prophets] and sent into the world [God ordained and sent many prophets unto the nations]; [Yeshua continues] Will you say that I blaspheme because I say [not that I am God] – that I am the Son of God?" (Thus ends the commentary on John 10:30-36.)

At his immersion, the moment was to the sensitive soul of Yeshua almost overwhelming. He felt that the very heavens opened and that a voice said, "Thou art my beloved son, in thee I am well pleased."

He had long called God "Father"; now he felt that God had called him "Son." It set the seal upon his mission. He believed that now the very spirit of God was in him, that it had descended upon his immersed head as gently as a dove.

In Yeshua the spiritual consciousness was developed until it permeated his entire personality and he could say in moments of exaltation, "I and my Father are one." This was not a statement to be interpreted theologically, but psychologically.

In conclusion, Yeshua called himself the son of God for

the two main reasons pointed out in John 10:30-36: (1) "Because he was the one in his day to whom the word of God came," and (2) "that the Father [God] had sanctified him and sent him into the world." Yeshua's reference to himself as the Son of God was strictly spiritual, and was in no way akin to the Greek-Roman-Catholic Church creation of the impregnation of Mary by God or by the Spirit of God, which they say is one and the same.

Yeshua lived like a son of God by precept and example. It is Christian theology, however, that has made him the unique and only begotten Son of God, completely equal to the Almighty.

Black man, Black woman, you have the "Jesus" and the religion that was given to you in slavery by the slavemaster.

WE HAVE BEEN GREATLY DECEIVED!

Chapter 8

THE UNACCEPTABILITY OF "THE DOCTRINE OF ORIGINAL SIN"

HAVE ALL HUMANS WHO HAVE EVER LIVED, all who are living now, and all who will ever live, forever be the victims of a curse because of Adam's transgression? The "Doctrine of Original Sin" says "YES!"

Christianity teaches that when Adam sinned he and, subsequently, all mankind were cursed by God, and only the shedding of Jesus' blood through his death on the cross (4,000 years later) redeemed Man back to God. Christianity further decrees that only by accepting the Lord Jesus Christ as the Son of God and as one's personal Saviour can one be saved.

Read the Adam and Eve story in the Bible for yourself; don't take anyone else's word for it. It appears in portions of Genesis chapter 2-5. You will not see anywhere in the story or in the entire Old Testament narrative where Adam or Eve were cursed. That they were cursed is only an assumption and part of the deceit and foolery which we have been discussing throughout this book. Of the three characters in the story – Adam, Eve, and the Serpent – only the Serpent was cursed (Gen. 3:14). God also cursed the ground for Adam's sake (3:17). Later, however, because of Noah's righteousness, after the Flood God rescinded the curse which He had placed upon the ground (8:21). As for Adam and Eve, they were punished, not cursed (3:16, 17, 23, 24).

There is a difference in definition between "punished" and "cursed." Your child disobeys, say, breaks the rules of your home; do you punish him or curse him? Of all the synonyms in Webster's Collegiate Dictionary for the word "punish" (chastise, castigate, chasten, discipline, correct), "curse" is not one of them.

Neither Adam nor Eve was cursed! This is just another attempt to deceive. If God were to curse everyone who sins – taking into consideration that there are sins of commission and sins of omission – then the entire human race would be cursed, for the Scripture says, "There is not a just man upon the earth that doeth good and sinneth not" (Eccl. 7:20).

Why are millions the world over allowing themselves to be "led by the nose" spiritually? It's all right to question some things in the Bible; everything therein is not the divinely inspired Word of God – and that's Old and New Testaments alike. It's even all right to question the Almighty in some instances: Abraham, Moses, Job, David, Isaiah, Jeremiah, Habakkuk and Yeshua did, and were never chided by God for it.

Did Jesus Die For the Sins of All Mankind?

Nowhere in the message of Yeshua did he ever say, hint or suggest that he died for the sins of the trillions of people who have already lived, the seven billion who are living now, and the trillions yet unborn. This is the doctrine of Paul, and the Roman Catholic Church, the mother of all Christian churches.

This doctrine further espouses that "because of Adam's sin, all men became sinners. God therefore offered up His son Jesus as a sacrifice for the sins of Man." The Catholic Church and some other Christian churches have as a part of their belief system the ritual of Infant Baptism. They believe that "the infant is born in sin – or, is a sinner – because of Adam;

therefore the newborn must be baptized through sprinkling to expiate that sin." If Jesus' death was a sacrifice for sin, why, then, must an infant be sprinkled to take away sin?

God Is Against Human Sacrifice

There are several instances in the Hebrew Scriptures (Genesis through Malachi) where God speaks disdainfully concerning human sacrifice. Abraham knew the Most High as "El Shaddai" – Almighty God – and was commanded by Him to "Walk before Me, and be thou wholehearted" (perfect) (Gen. 17:1). As a test of his faith and obedience, Abraham was ordered to offer his son Isaac upon an altar for a burnt offering. When he would have slain him, he was instructed thusly by the Almighty: "Lay not thine hand upon the lad, neither do thou anything unto him . . ." (Gen. 22:12).

The Prophet Micah forbade the people in his day to engage in human sacrifice for sin, saying, ". . . Shall I give my first-born for my transgression, the fruit of my body [that is, one's children] for the sin of my soul?" Since God is against human sacrifice and would not allow Abraham to offer up <u>his</u> son, and instructed ancient Israel under Moses not to send their children through the fire as a sacrifice, why, then, would God offer up <u>His</u> son, Jesus, as a human sacrifice? as Christology affirms.

The story of the Binding of Isaac opens the age-long warfare of Israel against the abominations of child sacrifice, which was rife among the Semitic peoples, as well as their Egyptian neighbors. In that age it was astounding that Abraham's God should have interposed to prevent the sacrifice, not that He should have asked for it. A primary purpose of this command, therefore, was to demonstrate to Abraham and his descendants after him that God abhorred human sacrifice with an infinite abhorrence. Unlike the heathen deities, it was the spiritual surrender alone that God required.

Just What Was Yeshua's Purpose On Earth?

Enough unadulterated truth has been left in both the Old and New Testaments for those who are seeking Truth to still find their way. It is the indispensable duty of those who have spent their lives in biblical and historical research and have been taught bt a prophet to make the way so plain that none will ignorantly err.

There are many quotations of Yeshua in which he clearly states the purpose of his being, and in none of them does he relate that he came to die in order to blot out the 'Adamic curse' or to shed his blood for the salvation of all mankind. He gave his first recorded reason when he was just twelve years old, saying to his parents, "How is it that ye sought me? Knew ye not that *I must be about my Father's business?"* (Luke 2:49.) Shouldn't we all be about our Father's business – the business of truth, mercy and justice?

"For the Son of man is come to seek and to save that which was lost." Every prophet is sent by God for the very same reason – to save the people of his day, not through his flesh but through his message and example. Israel was lost – lost in Egyptian bondage; the Almighty sent Moses to seek and to save them. Jonah was sent by God to Nineveh to seek and to save the Ninevites. And so it is with every prophet.

Did Yeshua come to save the world? No. He said, "I am not sent but to [I am sent only to] *the lost sheep of the house of Israel"* (Matt. 15:24). Now we see who were the lost sheep in Yeshua's day – Israel; and True Israel is still lost today – destroyed for the lack of knowledge – because he has lost his God. Not only did Yeshua say that he was sent to the "lost sheep of the house of Israel," but he told his disciples, *"Go not into the way of the Gentiles . . ., but go rather to the lost sheep of the house of Israel* (Matt. 10:5, 6).

What are some of the other reasons for which Yeshua said he came? *"I must work the works of Him that sent me while it is day:* the night cometh, when no man can work" (John 9:4). *"I am come that they might have life, and that they might have it more abundantly"* (John 10:10). Every prophet brings "an abundant life" message, and that message comes through obedience to the will of God.

Did he come to destroy the Commandments (the Law) of God or the eternal truths established by the prophets of old? No, for he said, "Think not that I am come to destroy the Law, or the Prophets: I am not come to destroy, but to fulfill" (Matt. 5:17). (A synonym for *fulfill:* PERFORM.)

Did Yeshua come to send peace on earth? Did he come to restore harmony to the family? *"Think not,"* said he, *"that I am come to send peace on earth: I came not to send peace but a sword. For I am come to set a man at variance against his father, and the daughter against her mother, and the daughter in law against her mother in law."* (Matt. 10:34,35; Luke 12:49; 51-53.) The words of a prophet are sometimes disturbing, for he speaks forth the words that most people do not want to hear: "Thus saith the LORD God, 'Amend your ways and your doings.'"

"Remission of Sins"

Remission. Act of remitting; pardon; esp. remission of sin. (Webster.)

"Remission of Sins" may well be the most important and interesting subheading in this entire chapter.

The phrase, *remission of sins,* appears only four times within the text of the Gospels: once in Matthew, once in Mark, and twice in Luke. Only in <u>one</u> instance – Matthew – is it stated that *"the blood of Jesus is shed for the remission of sins."* Neither Mark, Luke nor John record <u>anything</u> about the blood of Jesus in reference to the remission of sins, but rather they cite the performance of <u>another</u> major obligation as the criteria for absolution of sins, as we shall discover.

Let us now engage in a critical analysis of these four passages, and see if we can bring forth an even better understanding of Yeshua's mission.

MATTHEW 26:27, 28 – *"And he took the cup, and gave thanks, and gave it to them, saying, Drink all ye of it; For this is my blood of the new testament, which is shed for many for the remission of sins."*

The scene is Yeshua's last Passover, which most Christians refer to as "the Last Supper." Although the words in this passage are attributed to Yeshua, we refuse to believe that this quotation is actually his, and we have good reasons to support our position. As an Israelite, he would never command, even symbolically, that his disciples "drink his blood." The drinking of blood was a pagan practice and had been a ritual among heathen nations for many centuries. Furthermore, blood consumption among God's people had been forbidden since Noachal times, as this was one of the Seven Precepts of Noah, issued to him by God. This prohibition carried over into the Mosaic period and far beyond. As pointed out in the chapter, *There Are Two Jesuses In the New Testament,* "The Gospels carry many expressions in red (in Red Letter Edition Bibles) that Yeshua did not say, but were placed there by the powers of the times to deceive the world and create a 'second' and 'false' Jesus." We contend that Matthew 26:27, 28 is one of many such passages.

If Yeshua saw himself as the ultimate in salvation for all mankind – past, present and future – why, then, <u>didn't he</u> in his many parables, sermons and story-tellings just hammer that theme over and over again. Rather, the main focus of his three-year ministry was on bringing men and women to the knowledge and the doing of the will of God. He said in John 4:22, in his conversation with the woman at the well, "Ye worship ye know not what: we know what we worship; <u>for salvation is of the Jews."</u> What Yeshua is emphatically stating here is that you will find salvation through the Sinai Revelation and the teaching of the Prophets – the way of life which God gave to the Israelites (Jews?). He did not say that salvation is in the shedding of his blood on Calvary. Again, we must therefore look to the doctrine of Paul, the Greco-Roman Empire, and the Roman Catholic Church as the originators and promulgators of this dogma.

What do the writers of Mark and Luke record as a requirement *for the remission of sins?*

MARK 1:4 – "John did baptize in the wilderness, and preach <u>the baptism of repentance for the remission of sins.</u>"

LUKE 1:76-77 – "And thou, child, shalt be called the prophet of the Highest: for thou shalt go before the face of the Lord to prepare his ways; <u>to give knowledge of salvation unto His people by the remission of their sins, through the tender mercy of our God . . ."</u>

LUKE 3:3 – "And he came into all the country about Jordan, preaching <u>the baptism of repentance for the remission of sins.</u>"

All three of the above passages speak of John the Baptist and his mission herein is made clear: "To make God's people aware of the necessity of salvation, not just through the baptism of water – which is only symbolic – but through the <u>baptism of repentance,</u> which is of the heart and soul.

Just Why Was Yeshua (Jesus) Crucified?

Was the crucifixion of Yeshua for the salvation of mankind, or was it political? The Romans had been crucifying people for hundreds of years before the birth of Yeshua. They had two methods of capital punishment: the guillotine for beheading and the cross for crucifying. King Herod had already beheaded John the Baptist for arousing the populace, drawing great crowds and speaking against the status quo of the Roman government. Right on John's heels came Jesus. He, too, like John, was seen as a rebel against Rome, and the Romans determined that they must get rid of him as they had John.

They gave Yeshua a trial and found him guilty on a trumped-up charge; because they saw him as a threat to Rome, they administered capital punishment. In other words, the death of Yeshua was another prophet being killed for the cause of righteousness and for the word of God.

Yeshua was not the only prophet who gave his life for the cause of righteousness. "O Jerusalem, Jerusalem," he bewails, "thou that killest the prophets, and stonest them which are sent unto you . . ." (Matt. 23:37). Elijah the prophet complained of how Ahab and Jezebel had slain God's prophets with the sword, and would have killed one hundred more had not Obadiah hid them in a cave. The Prophet Zechariah was stoned to death; Isaiah the prophet, says history, was sawed asunder, and Prophet Jeremiah was cast into a dungeon of miry clay (quicksand) to die. All this because they stood for righteousness. And so it was with Yochanan (John) the Proselytizer and Yeshua (Jesus) of Nazareth.

If Jesus died for the sins of all mankind – the dead, the living and the yet to live – how is it that such men as Noah, Abraham, and Job were able to attain a state of perfection and find favor in the sight of God long before Yeshua's time? Of course, these are by no means the only names among the righteous of biblical times; there were many among the just in those days as there are in every age.

The Doctrine of Original Sin – the idea that "all are under a curse because of Adam's disobedience" – is totally unacceptable. If God is all-wise and full of mercy – and He is – He would certainly not forever curse the crowning work of His creation – Mankind – for the sin of one individual.

Animal Sacrifice Later Forbidden By the Prophets

It is true that in the days of Moses the blood of certain animals and fowl was commanded by God as atonement for sin. This, however, was not an end but a means to an end. Remember, Israel was still young as a nation, just out of several centuries of rigorous bondage and not yet converted. The use of blood, representing life, in the rites of atonement symbolized the complete yielding up of the worshipper's life to God, and conveyed the thought that the surrender of a man to the will of God carried with it the assurance of Divine pardon.

Many years later, the Psalmist as well as the Classical Prophets succeeding Moses not only lessened but forbade the offering of animals as atonement for sin. More and more they placed the emphasis upon works of righteousness and a right spirit toward the Divine Being and one's fellowman.

We offer the following scriptures as proof of the foregoing claim:

Psalm 40:6 –

"Sacrifice and offering Thou didst not desire; mine eyes hast Thou opened; burnt offering and sin offering hast Thou not required. I delight to do Thy will, O my God; yea, Thy law is within my heart."

Isaiah 1:11, 18, 19 –

"To what purpose is the multitude of your sacrifices unto Me? saith the LORD: I am full of the burnt offerings of rams, and the fat fed beasts; and I delight not in the blood of bullocks, or of lambs, or of he goats. Wash you, make you clean; put away the evil of your doings from before mine eyes; cease to do evil; learn to do well; seek judgment, relieve the oppressed, judge the fatherless…and the widow."

Jeremiah 7:21-23 –

"Thus saith the LORD of hosts, the God of Israel; Put your burnt offerings unto your sacrifices, and eat flesh. For I spake not to your fathers, nor commanded them in the day that I brought them out of the land of Egypt, concerning burnt offerings or sacrifices: but this thing commanded I them, saying, Obey my voice, and I will be your God, and ye shall be my people; and walk ye in all My ways that I have commanded you, that it may be well with you."

Amos 5:14, 15, 21-24 –

"Seek good, and not evil; that ye may live: and so the LORD, the God of hosts, shall be with you, as you have spoken. Hate the evil, and love the good, and establish judgment in the gate; . . . I hate, I despise your feast days, and I will not smell in your solemn assemblies. Though ye offer Me burnt offerings, I will not accept them: neither will I regard the peace offerings of your fat beasts. But let judgment run down as waters, and righteousness like a mighty stream."

Micah 6:6-8 –

"Wherewith shall I come before the LORD, and bow myself before the high God? shall I come before him with burnt offerings, and with calves of a year old? Will the LORD be pleased with thousands of rams, or with ten thousands of rivers of oil? shall I give my firstborn for my transgression, the fruit of my body for the sin of my soul? He hath shown thee, O man, what is good, and what doth the LORD require of thee, but to do justly, and to love mercy, and to walk humbly with thy God?"

The keeping of God's Holy Commandments (which embraces love of the Creator and one's neighbor), confessing of sins to Him, the asking of forgiveness, and repentance of sins, coupled with prayer and good deeds, are ways by which men can find favor with God.

The Most High, through His servants the prophets, has made the way plain and simple, as the Prophet Isaiah proclaims: "Let the wicked forsake his way, and the unrighteous man his thoughts: and let him return unto the LORD, and He will have mercy upon him: and to our God, for He will abundantly pardon" (Isa. 55:7).

Our pen has been that of a ready writer,
undergirded with Truth from the Sacred Volume –
Truth which we trembled not to recall!

Chapter 9

ALLEGED CHRISTOLOGICAL REFERENCES IN SCRIPTURE

PROBABLY SINCE THE ADVENT OF MANKIND upon the earth, people have endeared their heroes, sometimes even to the brink of idolatry.

This chapter will expose, disqualify, challenge, annul, rebut and explain a host of Old Testament and New Testament scriptures which Christianity alleges are prophecies and the fulfillment of prophecies foretelling the pre-existence of Jesus, his immaculate conception and virgin birth, his death, burial, resurrection and ascension.

Some may see this and other chapters in this book as an attack on Jesus. Quite the contrary; our respect for the great contributions which Jesus has made to humanity has been expressed over and over again in this work. Rather than an attack, this book is a partial fulfillment of our obligation to contribute to the destruction of myths and the re-establishment of Spiritual Truths and Righteousness amongst men. Modern-day Christians are not responsible for the institution of these beliefs and the misinterpretation of these ancient scriptures. Such concepts began to develop as early as about 50 C.E. (A.D.) through the writings of Paul, and were later demanded by the civil powers of those times. Jesus was no longer on earth to help keep the record straight, for were he still among them he would not have allowed them to make of him a deity.

Again, the object of this book is not to offend, but to enlighten. However, the truth must be told.

The Creation of the Universe and Man

Who helped the Almighty God create the universe? Or, who was with Him during the Creation? The answer to one or both of these questions by most Christians is: JESUS." Yet, Genesis 1:1 states, "In the beginning GOD created the heaven and the earth." Their answer is based on the wrong 1:1 (on John 1:1 instead of Genesis 1:1). (Commentary on John chapter 1 will be seriously discussed later in this chapter.)

Throughout the Torah (the first five books), the Prophets and the Writings, God Almighty is God alone, and there is none like unto Him. In the Book of Deuteronomy (32:39) the Most High speaks through his servant Moses: *"See now that I, even I, am He, and there is no god with Me."* In the 40th chapter of Isaiah (vs. 12-14) the prophet presents a masterpiece on the omnipotence, the omnipresence and the omniscience of the Eternal One:

"Who hath measured the waters in the hollow of his hand, and meted out heaven with a span, and comprehended the dust of the earth in a measure, and weighed the mountains in scales, and the hills in a balance? Who hath directed the spirit of the LORD, or being His counsellor hath taught Him? With whom took He counsel, and who instructed Him, and taught Him in the path of judgment, and showed to Him the way of understanding?"

Verses 18 and 25:

"To whom then will ye liken God? or what likeness will ye compare unto Him? To who then will ye liken Me, or shall I be equal? saith the Holy One."

This is among the grandest passages in the Holy Writ.

The Creator declares further (Isaiah 42:8):

"I am the LORD: that is My name: and My glory will I not give to another, neither My praise to graven images."

According to Scripture, once again, did the Divine Being alone bring into existence the entire universe and all that is therein (including man), or did He have assistance? The answer can be found in the Book of the Prophet Isaiah (44:23):

"Thus saith the LORD thy redeemer, and He that formed thee from the womb; 'I am the LORD that maketh all things; that stretcheth forth the heavens <u>alone;</u> that spreadest abroad the earth <u>by Myself.</u>'"

It is believed by millions around the globe that when God said, "Let us make man in our image, after our likeness . . ." (Gen. 1:26), that He was talking to Jesus. Truthfully, no one knows to whom God was speaking, if to anyone at all. It could have merely been an expression of the writer of the chapter, because everywhere else where the creation of man is mentioned – and it appears in several places – God says, "I" [not "we"] created man. Many are the times when a speaker or writer will use the first person plural "we" or "us." In fact, "we" has been used exclusively throughout this book, even though it is the work of one author. If the Almighty needed help or guidance in bringing forth the Creation, then He would not be the Almighty.

Genesis 1:27 says, "So GOD created man . . ." No one else is mentioned! Genesis 2:7 also states: "And the LORD God formed man . . ."

Please allow us to speculate a little:

Since God formed man of the dust of the ground (2:7), the "Let us" (in 1:26) could be "God, and all the minerals, chemicals and vitamins that are in the earth, of which the human body is composed, as well as the sun (body warmth) and the air. Calcium, potassium, iron, phosphate, sodium, zinc and many other mineral, chemicals and vitamins are all in the bowels of Mother Earth; all that we eat comes from the earth, and man himself comes from the earth. Could it be, then, that God was speaking to those aforementioned components when He said "Let us [Me and Earth, etc.] make man"?

On the Immaculate Conception and Virgin Birth

The accounts of Mary's conception and Jesus' birth recorded in Matthew 1:18-23 and Luke 1:26-31 are neither in harmony with nor do they concur with the prophecy fulfillment reference presented by Christology from Isaiah 7:14. Yeshua (Jesus) had a natural father, as did each of us, and the passage in Isaiah has been taken entirely out of context and applied to Yeshua, as we shall discover, The Virgin Birth story is a part of Greek and Roman mythology, which Yeshua himself would never have recognized.

Matthew 1:18-23 reads as follows:

"Now the birth of Jesus Christ was on this wise: When as his mother Mary was espoused to Joseph, before they came together, she was found with child of the Holy Ghost. Then Joseph her husband, being a just man, and not willing to make her a public example, was minded to put her away privily. But while he thought on these things, behold, an angel of the Lord appeared unto him in a dream, saying, Joseph, thou son of David, fear not to take unto thee Mary thy wife: for that which is conceived in her is of the Holy Ghost. And she shall bring forth a son, and thou shalt call his name JESUS: for he shall save his people from their sins. Now all this was done, that it might be fulfilled which was spoken of the Lord by the prophet, saying, Behold, a virgin shall be with child, and shall bring forth a son, and they shall call his name Emmanuel, which being interpreted is, God with us."

Christianity teaches that the verses above (Matt. 1:18-23) are the fulfillment of the prophecy of Isaiah 7:14: but they are not! Isaiah 7:14 (KJV) states:

"Therefore the LORD Himself shall give you a sign: Behold, a virgin shall conceive and bear a son, and shall call his name Immanuel."

First of all, the Catholic Bible and the King James Version (KJV) are two of the few that carry the word "virgin." The encyclopedia states that King James wrote with Catholic tendencies. After all, he did inherit the Church of England from Henry VIII who was once a Catholic. King Henry broke away from Catholicism in 1534 because the Church would not grant him a divorce. He then established the Church of England, which is the same as the Episcopal Church in the United States. Though King James did not actually write the KJV, he authorized and sanctioned it. The Holy Hebrew Scriptures, the Good News Bible and the Jehovah's Witness Bible – the latter two of which are Christian in origin – all render Isaiah 7:14 as "a young woman" instead of "a virgin." The word *virgin* is an insertion by the Catholic Church and the writers of the KJV.

Irrespective of the terminology, however, the main point is that Isaiah 7:14 has absolutely nothing to do with the conception and birth of Jesus. In order to put the verse under discussion within its proper context, one must read with understanding the entire seventh chapter of Isaiah and the first ten verses of chapter eight in order to get the full meaning of Isaiah 7:14. The son spoken of in 7:14 is born in chapter 8:3. The question will arise, Why is it that in 7:14 it says, ". . . and shall call his name Immanuel," yet when the child is born (8:3), the LORD said to Isaiah, "Call his name Ma-her-shal-al-hash-baz." The answer is: In 7:14, "Immanuel" is given as the son's "significant" name, not as his given name – *"as a sign of the LORD's favor";* and the meaning of the name Immanuel is *"God* is *with us"* (8:10), not "God with us" (Matt. 1:23), which sets forth the false concept that Jesus was God in human flesh. Isaiah's son's given name, Ma-her-shal-al-hash-baz, on the other hand, signified that "Damascus and Samaria were soon to be plundered by the king of Assyria." Put both the significant name and his given name together – "Im-manuel" and "Ma-her-shal- al-hash-baz" – and we have "God is with us [Israel] in the plunder and defeat of Damascus and Samaria," the two countries which had conspired with each other to conquer Jerusalem (Isaiah 7:1-9).

Another example of a significant name appears in Jeremiah 23:5-6:

> "Behold, the days come, saith the LORD, that I will raise unto David a righteous branch, and a king shall reign and prosper, and shall execute judgment and justice in the earth. In his days Judah shall be saved, and Israel shall dwell safely: and this is the name whereby he shall be called, THE LORD OUR RIGHTEOUSNESS" (a significant name).

(The Hebrew Scriptures carries "THE LORD IS OUR RIGHTEOUSNESS.") The word *is* is omitted again in this verse in many Christian Bibles, as it is in Isaiah 7:14. **Special note from the Author:** When Jeremiah 23:5-6 speaks of the *righteous branch,* and then later in the same verse of *Judah and Israel,* it is not the *righteous branch* whom the Most High is saying *"shall be called 'THE LORD IS OUR RIGHTEOUSNESS,'"* but rather it is *Judah and Israel,* as one people, who shall *significantly* be so-called. Christianity inaccurately interprets this verse as a prophecy relating to Jesus, saying that he is the righteous branch to whom the passage refers. *(This is a revision on Jer. 23:5-6 to the earlier printings of this book.)*

Matthew 1 says that "Mary was with child of the Holy Ghost" (vs. 18). (Holy Ghost," "Holy Spirit," "Spirit of God" and "Spirit of the LORD" are all synonymous with most Christians.) Why would Jesus have to come into the world in an unnatural way? Is sex wicked? The Holy Spirit was not assigned to impregnate a woman; that is one of the functions which the Creator has given to Man, and Man continues to do an excellent job of it! One may argue, "With God all things are possible." We agree; but God does not cause the performance of a miracle without a reason. The parting of the Red Sea, the standing still of the sun, the deliverance of the three Hebrew children from the fiery furnace and Daniel from the den of lions, and the raising of the dead by Elijah were all done for a reason. We have yet to hear a sound reason for the immaculate conception and virgin birth of Jesus; only, "with

God all things are possible."

One could easily contend that the prophet Jeremiah was immaculately conceived and born of a virgin. God declares (Jer. 1:5), "Before I formed thee in the belly I knew thee . . ." It would be absurd to believe that God literally shaped Jeremiah in his mother's womb and that he did not have a biological father. Furthermore, anyone has yet to show either in the books of Matthew or Luke, or from any other source, where the Almighty God Himself or Yeshua ever said that he was immaculately conceived and born of a virgin.

Yeshua told Nicodemus, "That which is born of the flesh is flesh, and that which is born of the Spirit is spirit" (John 3:6). Therefore, flesh begets flesh, and Spirit begets spirit. Yeshua was flesh, begotten by flesh.

In five places in the Gospels it is clearly pointed out that the people who lived in the time of Yeshua – who knew, loved, walked and talked with him – proclaimed Joseph as his father.

In Matthew 13:55 –
"Is not this the carpenter's son? Is not his mother called Mary? and his brethren, James, and Joses, and Simon, and Judas? And his sisters, are they not all with us?"

In Luke 2:48 (last part) –
"And his mother said unto him, 'Behold, thy father and I have sought thee sorrowing.'"

In Luke 4:22 –
"And all bear him witness, and wondered at the gracious words which proceeded out of his mouth. And they said, Is not this the carpenter's son?"

In John 6:42 –
"And they said, Is not this Jesus, the son of Joseph, whose father and mother we know . . .?"

We shall further see what that Triune power was capable of, as far as taking scriptures out of context is concerned, when we examine the discrepancies in Matthew chapter 2. The

Immaculate Conception and Virgin Birth story is a creation of the Greeks, the Romans and the Roman Catholic Church.

O.T. Scriptures Fail to Fulfill in Matthew 2

There is now proof positive that the books of Matthew, Mark, Luke, and John were not written by them, and most modern-day historians agree. Mark is the earliest Gospel, but the man Mark was not a disciple of Yeshua, and neither was Luke (a Caucasian companion of Paul). (See Matthew 10:2-4, and you will discover that neither the names of Mark nor Luke are mentioned as disciples. Luke and Paul never saw Yeshua.)

From Cruden's Bible Dictionary comes this account:

"THE NEW TESTAMENT consists of four Gospels, the Acts of the Apostles, 21 Epistles, and the Revelation. All of these books were written within the second century after Christ, but between two and three more centuries passed before the Canon was finally settled. This was done by the Councils of Laodicea (A.D. 369), Hippo Regius (A.D. 393), and Carthage (A.D. 397). All Christian churches agree on this important point and have the same New Testament, though in different versions."

A lot of changing, editing, "fixing," tampering and bickering went on during those two or three centuries by the powers of the times before the New Testament was finalized.

There are serious discrepancies in Matthew chapter 2; in three places the supposed fulfillments are not in accord with the Old Testament scriptures which are referenced.

1. Matthew 2:14-15 –

"When he arose, he took the young child and his mother by night, and departed into Egypt: and was there until the death of Herod: that it might be fulfilled which was spoken of the Lord by the prophet, saying, 'Out of Egypt have I called my son.'"

The supposed prophetic reference for Joseph bringing Yeshua out of Egypt (vs. 15, ". . . out of Egypt have I called My son") is Hosea 11:1. But God, in Hosea, was not speaking of a future event, but of a past one. *"When Israel was a child, then I loved him, and called My son out of Egypt"* (11:1).

INTERPRETATION: *"When Israel was a child"* (an enslaved people in Egypt, in their infancy – not even then a nation) *"then I* [God] *loved him* [Israel], *and called* [through Moses] *My son* [Israel] *out of Egypt."* (See also Ex. 4:22.23 for Israel as God's son.)

Matthew 2:16-18 –

"Then Herod, when he saw that he was mocked of the wise men, was exceeding wroth, and sent forth, and slew all the children that were in Bethlehem, and in all the coasts thereof, from two years old and under . . . Then was fulfilled that which was spoken by Jeremy the prophet, saying, In Rama was there a voice heard, lamentation, and weeping, and great mourning, Rachel weeping for her children, and would not be comforted, because they are not."

The supposed prophetic reference for the killing of all children two years and under by Herod, and the weeping in Rama by Rachel for her children (Matt. 2:16-18), is Jeremiah 31:15, which reads as follows:

"Thus saith the Lord: A voice was heard in Ramah, lamentation, and bitter weeping; Rahel [Rachel] weeping for her children refused to be comforted for her children, because they were not."

Verse 16 reads:

"Thus saith the LORD: Refrain thy voice from weeping, and thine eyes from tears: for thy work shall be rewarded, saith the LORD; and they shall come again from the land of the enemy."

INTERPRETATION: Both verses (Jer. 31:15, 16) are telling of the distressful times experienced by the Israelites in the days of Jeremiah when Nebuchadnezzar overthrew Jerusalem and carried the people captive to Babylon. Ramah was a city of the Benjamite tribe where those captured by Nebuchadnezzar – men, women and children – were held prisoner before being carried off to Babylon. The mothers, here represented as Rachel ("Rahel"), one of the matriarchs of Israel and mother of Benjamin, were bitterly weeping over their children's fate; no one was able to comfort them at that time.

But wait! God offers hope (verse 16, above). He promises a reward for their work and a return from the land of their enemies (Babylon). Jeremiah 31:15,16, therefore, is in no way a prophecy relating to Matthew 2:16-18.

3. Matthew 2:23 –

"And he [Jesus] came and dwelt in a city called Nazareth, that it might be fulfilled which was spoken by the prophets, He shall be called a Nazarene."

The Old Testament reference set forth by Christian biblical historians as a fulfillment of Matthew 2:23, is Judges 13:5. But again, it does not concur with the text in Matthew. INTER-PRETATION: *"And he* [Jesus] *came and dwelt in a city called Nazareth.* Neither "Nazareth" nor "Nazarene" appears anywhere within the text of the Old Testament. How, then, could Matthew 2:23 state, *". . . that it might be fulfilled which was spoken by the prophet, 'He shall be called a Nazarene'"?* The reference offered in Judges 13:5 is really an announcement of the birth of Samson: that he shall be a <u>Nazarite</u> – which has no connection whatsoever to "Nazareth" or "Nazarene." Samson was to drink neither wine nor strong drink, and no razor was to come upon his head. Therefore, he was a lifetime <u>Nazarite</u> from his mother's womb.

Yeshua (Jesus) was a "Nazarene" because he was raised in "Nazareth" (Luke 4:16), but there is no such quotation as "he shall be called a Nazarene" anywhere in scripture from Genesis to Malachi.

So you see that all of the aforementioned Old Testament references, and hundreds more too numerous to cite, have been taken out of context and applied to Yeshua, not by Yeshua but by the early Gentile Church fathers who distorted many quotations from the Hebrew Scriptures in compiling and canonizing the New Testament, with the intent to deceive.

Some of the other most misunderstood and misinterpreted scriptures are Isaiah 9:6, Isaiah chapter 53, and John chapter 1.

Yeshua Himself Would Frown on John Chapter 1

John chapter 1 is blasphemous! especially verses 1-18. The disciple John could not possibly have written it.

The New Testament on the whole does not seem to carry the weight and impact that is carried in the Old. After you pass the "Sermon On the Mount," which includes Matthew chapters 5, 6 and 7, and the other pure teaching of Yeshua, there is very little, if any, documentation that God revealed to the writers their various messages. In the Hebrew Scriptures (O.T.) the prophecies of the prophets are invariably prefaced with such phrases as: "And the LORD spake unto Moses and Aaron, saying, . . ."; "Thus saith the LORD God . . ."; "And the word of the LORD came unto me, saying, . . .; "Then said the LORD unto me . . ."; "The word which came unto Jeremiah from the LORD, saying, . . .; etc. Following the preface the prophets then proceed to tell what the Most High revealed to them. What we see in the Gospels is simply, "The Gospel According To Saint Matthew," "The Gospel According To Saint Mark," "The Gospel According To Saint Luke," "The Gospel According To Saint John," with no documented proof whatsoever that their accounts were revealed to them by the Almighty. Where is the "Thus saith the LORD God" in the Greek Scriptures (N.T.)?

All of Paul's Epistle's were just that – epistles – letters to the Gentiles at Greece and Rome, and are not to be equated in any way with the Divine Revelations of the prophets from Moses through Malachi. John chapter 1 is no exception.

The Fallacies of John 1, Verses 1, 2, 3, 10, 14 & 17

VERSE 1. *"In the beginning was the Word, and the Word was with God, and the Word was God"*: This verse is mind-boggling. In the beginning was the Word? This is in sharp conflict with Genesis 1:1–"In the beginning GOD...! No one else. Nothing else – but darkness and chaos. *"And the Word was with God, and the Word was God":* How can something be "with God" and "be God" at the same time?

VERSE 2. *"The same was in the beginning with God":* The Divine Being said, **"There is no god with Me"** (Deut. 32:39).

VERSE 3: *"All things were made by him; and without him was not anything made that was made":* Now we are really confused. All things were made by whom? By God, or by the Word? We agree that God *spoke* the word: "Let there be…and there was…" Or did He really *speak* at all? Maybe the Almighty just *willed* it, and it all came into being – in six days – not in six 24-hour periods, but in six stages of time.

VERSES 6-10. *"There was a man sent from God, whose name was John. The same came to bear witness of the Light, that all men through him might believe* (vss. 6,7). *He was in the world, and the world was made by him, and the world knew him not":* Hundreds of millions of people had been believing in God long before John and Yeshua were born. Yeshua was not the only person who was the light; he told the people of God in his day, "<u>Ye</u> are the light of the world…" Of himself he said, "<u>As long as I am in the world, I am the light of the world</u> (John 9:5). Jesus is no longer in the world. In 1:10 the writer is speaking of Jesus when he says, *"He was in the world, and the world was made by him."* Is he serious? The world was made by the Creator God! Moses, the foremost of all the prophets, should know. In Psalm 90:1,2 – *A Prayer of Moses the Man of God* – he declares: "LORD, Thou hast been our dwelling place in all generations. Before the mountains were brought forth or ever [before] <u>Thou hadst formed the earth and the world,</u> even from everlasting to everlasting,

Thou art God." So we see here who made the world.

VERSE 14: *"And the Word was made flesh..."* If "the Word was God" (vs. 1), and then "the Word was made flesh," the writer is then saying that "God became flesh." The prophets of old and Yeshua taught that "God is Spirit," not flesh (Isaiah 31:3, John 4:24).

VERSE 17. *"For the law was given by Moses, but grace and truth came by Jesus Christ."* It is true that the law was given by Moses, but how ridiculous it is to say that *"grace and truth came by Jesus Christ!"* Webster's Collegiate Dictionary carries as the foremost definition for "grace" the following: "Favor, kindness, mercy," etc. Are you telling us, Mr. Writer of John chapter 1, that there was no favor, no kindness and no mercy in the world from God or man for the 4,000 years that preceded Yeshua? No truth, either, until the advent of Yeshua? The only scriptures that Yeshua knew was the so-called "Old Testament," and he lived thereby and often quoted therefrom. They contained then and today the TRUTH of the Almighty through His prophets.

An attempt has been made in John chapter 1 and in other places in the so-called New Testament to overthrow and destroy all that the former holy prophets and other inspired teachers and writers have established over the forty centuries predating Yeshua: (that) "the Creator alone is God, and beside Him there is no other."

The "New Testament" is known universally as "the Greek Scriptures." It just seemed impossible for the Greeks and Romans to conceptualize the idea of One Unseen Almighty Creator. They had worshipped many gods and goddesses for centuries. All seven days of the week and the first six months of the year on the Gregorian/Roman Calendar are named after Greek, Roman, and German gods and goddesses.

When Paul went to Greece and introduced the people there to the knowledge of the Divine Being, he presented it to them in a "watered down" form. Both the Greeks and the Romans were used to gods they could see, so Paul gave them his creation of "a Saviour God who had become man, who had died, and who had been resurrected, and all who believed in him would be saved." Paintings and statues of Jesus and Mary eventually began to appear on the edifices of churches which Paul had established in various Greek cities, such as Corinth, Ephesus, Galatia, Thessalonica, Colosse, and Philippi. To further appease the Gentiles, the introduction of the Triune God – God the Father, God the Son, and God the Holy Ghost (which later became known as the Trinity) – was allowed, contrary to all that the prophets, including Yeshua, had taught.

From the foregoing, it is very understandable how these world powers, under whose control the New Testament writing fell, were able to adulterate the pure teaching of Yeshua and those who succeeded him who had been schooled in the way of the prophets.

Isaiah 9:6-7 – "For Unto Us a Child is Born . . ."

What is referred to as "the Old Testament" is known universally as the *Hebrew Scriptures,* and the defenders of our faith in every generation refuse to deem the Greek and Roman Church fathers of the first three centuries C.E. (A.D.) qualified to interpret our Sacred Scriptures.

For centuries now, rabbis Black and White, who have interpreted Isaiah 9:6,7 to be a prophetic reference to Hezekiah son of Ahaz, king of Israel.

The King James Version's (KJV) rendering of Isaiah 9:6,7 is quite different from that found in the Hebrew Holy Scriptures – English translation.

Let us now compare the two renderings , and then offer an interpretation from the foremost Judaic commentary:

FROM THE KING JAMES VERSION: *"For unto us a child is born, unto us a son is given: and the government shall be upon his shoulder: and his name shall be called Wonderful, Counsellor, The mighty God, The everlasting Father, The Prince of Peace. Of the increase of his government and peace there shall be no end, upon the throne of David, and upon his kingdom, to order it, and to establish it with judgment and with justice from henceforth and for ever. The zeal of the LORD of hosts will perform this"* (Isa. 9:6,7).

FROM THE HEBREW SCRIPTURES: *"Unto us a child has been born, unto us a son has been given: and the government is upon his shoulder; and his name is called †Pele-joez-el-gibbor-abi-ad-sar-shalom; That the government may be increased, and of peace there be no end, even upon the throne of David, and upon his kingdom, to establish it, and to uphold it through justice and through righteousness from henceforth even for ever. The zeal of the LORD of hosts doth perform this"* (Isa. 9:6, 7).

INTERPRETATION: *"Unto us a child has been born, unto us a son has been given":* The prophetic reference here is to Hezekiah, then a lad when the prophecy was uttered. *"And the government is upon his shoulder":* This clearly indicates that the 'crown prince' – Hezekiah son of Ahaz – is the person to whom the prophecy refers. *"And his name is called pele-joez-el-gibbor-abi-ad-sar-shalom":* that is, "Wonderful in counsel is God the mighty, the Everlasting Father, the Ruler of peace." This is the "significant name" by which the child would be known. The KJV gives *"Wonderful, Counsellor, The*

---

†That is, Wonderful in counsel is God the mighty, the Everlasting Father, the Ruler of peace.

Mighty God, the everlasting Father, The Prince of Peace."
This is quite impossible. No true prophet – indeed, no true
Israelite – would apply a term like 'Mighty God' or
'everlasting Father' to any mortal prince.

"The throne of David" (vs. 7): The kingdom of Israel,
devastated by the Assyrians in the days of Ahaz, fell into the
hands of Hezekiah by reason of the weakening of Assyria in
his days. For the first time since the days of Solomon, the
national unity was re-established, and Hezekiah was the first
ruler once more to occupy the throne of David, hence the
Prophet speaks of the *increase of his government. "For
ever":* That is, during the entire lifetime of Hezekiah's reign.
"The zeal of the LORD of hosts": The love of God for His
people, and His passion for Righteousness, guarantee the
promised deliverance.

Hezekiah's righteous reign will lift Israel from the degen-
erate condition into which it had sunk. Hezekiah will be the
leader of the 'holy seed,' the indestructible faithful Remnant
in Israel.

Isaiah 53 – Ill-written and Misinterpreted

There is a serious problem with the "tenses" in the 53rd
chapter of Isaiah, as rendered in the KJV of the Bible. It
violates the rules of the English language when present tense,
past tense and future tense are all engaged at the same time in
the telling of an event. This is especially true with a prophecy
when it is foretelling that which is to come.

Biblical prophecies foretelling the future are prefaced with
such phrases as, "And it <u>shall</u> come to pass..." (Isa. 2:1-4);
and "I <u>will raise</u> again the tabernacle of David that is fallen..."
(Amos 9:11); also as in Daniel 7:25; 12:1,2, all of which were
foretelling future events from the time of their respective utter-

ances. There are hundreds of prophecies in scripture given in future tense. In Isaiah 53:2, both present and future tenses are employed in the same verse. In vss. 3-6 past and present tenses are used; vss. 7-9, past tense; vs. 10 is mixed with past and future tense; vs. 11 is future tense, and vs. 12 is past and future tenses combined. This chapter in the KJV is a literary disaster; King James and his 70 scholars should have been ashamed to have released it. (For an exhaustive commentary on Isaiah chapter 53, read our book entitled *A NON-CHRISTIAN'S RESPONSE TO CHRISTIANITY,* page 70.)

In the Hebrew Scriptures – English translation – the entire 53rd chapter of Isaiah is in past tense. The Prophet speaks of a person to whom the events of his message had already taken place. We cannot allow the Greeks, the Romans and the Catholic Church to interpret our Scriptures for us.

When we consider all of the foregoing in this chapter on *Alleged Christological References In Scripture,* we see just what the powers of yester-century have done in changing and misinterpreting the scriptures in order to authenticate the "new way" and destroy the "old paths" (Jer. 6:16; Dan. 7:25).

And what might the prophets and psalmists of old say, were they alive today to witness such a multitude of deceptions? Possibly, *"Look What They've Done To My Song!"*

"Drama often clouds the real issue."

Chapter 10

THE 'NEW COVENANT' OF JEREMIAH 31, AND PAUL'S MISINTERPRETATION OF IT

IN OUR LIFETIME we have discussed the subject, *"The New Covenant,"* with literally scores of people among our Christian acquaintances. All of them, without exception, have always reached the same conclusion (that): "With the shedding of Jesus' blood on the cross, the 'old covenant' was made null and void." Whenever Christian writers and other members of that persuasion discuss the annulment of the so-called *old covenant,* they actually say that all of the laws, statutes and judgments which God gave to ancient Israel through Moses, have been abolished. This includes, most of them agree, even The Ten Commandments. All of the above, they declare, is the old Mosaic Law which was eradicated by Christ, and a New Covenant has now been ushered in by him. Mainly responsible for this belief among millions are the writings of the Apostle Paul.

Herein lies the problem: When the Most High speaks of "a new covenant" in the 31st chapter of Jeremiah's prophecy, He is speaking of the Ten Commandments, as we shall see later on in this chapter. When Paul elaborates on Jeremiah's prophecy, he is referring to the ceremonial laws, which in Moses' time included sprinkling of the blood of animals upon the altar and the people; these were temporary laws, as thoroughly documented in the chapter, *"The Unacceptability of*

88

the Doctrine of Original Sin" (subheading, *Animal Sacrifice Later Forbidden By the Prophets,* page 69).

Let us now examine both texts – that of Jeremiah 31 and that of Paul in his Epistle to the Hebrews – and discover the inaccuracies and misinterpretations by the man who proclaimed himself as "the Apostle to the Gentiles."

Jeremiah 31:31-34 –

"Behold, the days come, saith the LORD, that I will make a new covenant with the house of Israel, and with the house of Judah: Not according to the covenant that I made with their fathers in the day that I took them by the hand to bring them out of the land of Egypt, which My covenant they brake [broke], although I was an husband unto them, saith the LORD: But this shall be the covenant that I will make with the house of Israel: After those days, saith the LORD, I will put My law in their inward parts, and write it in their hearts: and will be their God, and they shall be My people. And they shall teach no more every man his neighbour, and every man his brother, saying, Know the LORD: for they shall all know Me, from the least of them unto the greatest of them, saith the LORD: for I will forgive their iniquity, and I will remember their sin no more."

Hebrews 8:7-13 –

"For if the first [or old] covenant had been faultless, then should no place have been found for the second [or new]. For finding fault with them, he saith, Behold the days come, saith the Lord, when I shall make a new covenant with the house of Israel and with the house of Judah: Not according to the covenant that I made with their fathers when I took them by the hand to lead them out of the land of Egypt; because they continued not in my covenant, <u>and I regarded them not,</u> saith the Lord. For this is the covenant that I will make with the house of Israel, saith the Lord; I will put my law<u>s</u> into their mind, and write <u>them</u> in their hearts: and I will be to them a God, and they shall be to me a people: and they shall not teach every man his neighbour, and every man his brother, saying, Know the Lord: for all shall know me, from the least to the greatest. For I will be merciful to their unrighteousness, and their sins and their iniquities will I remember no more. In that he saith, A new covenant, he hath made the first old. Now that which decayeth and waxeth old is ready to vanish away."

First, notice the differences in the two renderings: Jeremiah 31:32 does not carry the phrase, *<u>"and I regarded them not"</u>* in any version of the Bible; Hebrews 8:9 does, and is, therefore, an addition. Jeremiah 31:33 carries the word "law";

Hebrews (8:10) carries "law<u>s</u>." There is a difference in Old Testament Scripture between "law" and "laws," as pertains to the Ten Commandments. The Commandments are not "ten laws," but one law with ten points. They are known in Scripture and in history by several other names: the Covenant, the Testimony, the Decalogue, the Ten Words, and the Sinai Revelation, and are not to be confused with the other "603 law<u>s</u>" recorded in the Torah (the first five books of the Bible). Many of those laws were not for all time, neither were all of them for each individual. There were laws for prophets, priests, Levites, kings, farmers, cooks, men, women, children, men of war, the infirm, etc., etc.

On the other hand, the Ten Commandments were for all of ancient Israel, and still remain till this day the standard of conduct for all mankind.

The "new covenant" which God through Jeremiah declared that He would make with Israel and Judah (Jer. 31:31-34) is not really a new covenant at all, but is the same "old covenant" which God promises to make <u>in a new way</u> – "in their inward parts and in their hearts." In verse 33, God says, *"But this shall be the covenant that I will make with the house of Israel; After those days, saith the LORD, I will put My law* [the same law] *in their inward parts, and write it in their hearts..."* The first time God wrote His law in the time of Moses, He wrote it upon two tables of stone. This is clearly pointed out in Exodus 24:12 and in Deuteronomy 4:12, 13 –

"And the LORD said unto Moses, Come up to Me into the mount, and be there: and I will give thee tables of stone, and a law [not law<u>s</u>] *and commandments which I have written; that thou mayest teach them"* (Exodus 24:12).

"And the LORD spake unto you out of the midst of the fire: ye heard the voice of the words, but saw no similitude; only ye heard a voice. And He declared unto you <u>His covenant,</u> which He commanded you to perform, even ten commandments; and He wrote them upon two tables of stone" (Deuteronomy 4:12, 13).

And why stone, rather than wood or paper? Stone symbolizes the permanence and perpetuity of the holy law of God.

Israel under Moses was young as a nation, really just a child (Hosea 11:1), and was not able on the whole, after 430 years' sojourn in Egypt, to receive the law of God into their hearts. Human nature just would not dictate that, as they had become almost totally Egyptianized. To show their importance, the Decalogue was thrice given: Exodus 20:3-17 in spoken form, and Exodus 24:12 and 34:1, in written form. In a subsequent and final writing of the Law, however, and in a different era the Almighty promises to put His Law – the same Law – in their inward parts and write it anew in their hearts. The Psalmist understood this clearly when he wrote: *"The mouth of the righteous speaketh wisdom, and his tongue talks of judgment. The Law of God is in his heart; none of his steps shall slide* (Psa. 37:30).

Jeremiah makes us to understand that once the law of God is in the hearts of men and women, boys and girls, it will no longer be necessary to go from neighbor to neighbor and from brother to brother, saying, "Know the LORD!" For when the heart, mind and soul are filled with the love of God and love of neighbor, which is the sum and substance of the Ten Commandments (Deut. 6:5, Lev. 19:18, Matt. 22:37-40), that will be the time when "they shall all know Me, from the least of them to the greatest of them."

Paul greatly "misses the boat" in Hebrews 8:7-14. He is speaking of a different covenant altogether than the prophet Jeremiah. Paul carries over from chapter 8 to chapter 9, and discusses the furniture of the tabernacle built in the wilderness under Moses' leadership. In 9:1 he mentions the "first covenant," which is the same as his use of the word "old" in 8:13. He is on an "entirely different page" than Jeremiah.

The prophets of the Hebrew Scriptures as well as Yeshua taught the Ten Commandments, and the Apostle James proclaims the Covenant as "the perfect law of liberty."

After Moses had received the Covenant from the Most High on two tables of stone, He commanded him to build an ark to house the Covenant. It is called to this day the Ark of the Covenant. Nothing else was placed inside th Ark but the Covenant. The other laws, which Moses himself wrote, were placed in the side of the Ark (Ex. 25:16,21; 40:20; Deut. 10:4,5; 31:24-26).

The Law of Ten Commandments is perfect, so much so, that if every man, woman and child of every nation, kindred, tongue and people would obey them to the best of their ability, then could every voice and every heart be lifted up in unison and resoundingly proclaim, "WHAT A WONDERFUL WORLD!!"

The New Testament was written mainly – though not entirely – to exalt Jesus as the Saviour of the world. God Almighty is the world's Saviour (Isaiah 45:22, and elsewhere), and He saves through His Commandments and through the message and teaching of His holy prophets. Yeshua was one of the prophets – no more and no less. There is some truth in the New Testament, but I declare unto you that Jesus was not and is not the Saviour of the world, he did not die for our sins, he is not in heaven, neither is he coming again. Read Matthew, Mark, Luke, and John, and you will not find anywhere where Yeshua said that he died for the sins of mankind! That story was created by Paul for the Gentiles of Greece and Rome.

THE ALMIGHTY WANTS US TO RETURN,
FOR WE HAVE BEEN GREATLY DECEIVED!

REMEMBER THE HOLOCAUST!
REMEMBER THE HOLOCAUST!

The

African Holocaust, That Is!

(West African Slave Trade: ca. 1517-1865)

Genocide Rape Castration Lynching Racism Injustice

"Without Ever Forgetting the Past, We Must Forge Ahead to the Future!"

93

BLACK HUMANS FOR SALE

Chapter 11

The Merchandise of Slaves, & Souls of Men

(The image to the left (page 94) depicts the miserable, cramped conditions of 510 Africans on board the bark <u>Wildfire,</u> who, while being smuggled into the United States in 1860, were captured by an anti-slaving vessel. The slaves were taken to Key West, Florida, and from there were sent to Liberia where the United States regularly repatriated "recaptured" Africans after 1808.)

THE FIRST CAPTURED SLAVES came to the Western Hemisphere in the early 1500s. Twenty African slaves were brought to Jamestown, Virginia, in 1619. A series of complex colonial laws began to regulate the status of Africans and their descendants to slavery. The United States outlawed the transatlantic slave trade in 1808, but the domestic slave trade and illegal importation continued for several decades.

Captured Africans were sold at auction as "chattel," like

HUMANS FOR SALE!
GUINEA:
To be sold . . . a cargo of 170 prime young likely healthy Guinea slaves.

---

inanimate property or animals. Many literate ex-slaves discussed the degradation and humiliation they felt when they were treated like "cattle."

The 1774 broadside, typical of the advertisements used in the North as well as the South before the Civil War, advertises the sale of slaves and land, the availability of employment for an overseer, a recall of debts, and a reward for anyone who captured two runaway slaves. The captors claim that the Angolan Africans, scheduled to be sold at auction in Savannah, Georgia, were "prime, young, likely healthy." The runaway advertisement on this same broadside gives specific information about two African-born male runaways which includes height, complexion, build, and clothing.

Slaves Commandeer The 'Creole'

In November1841 the 135 enslaved African Americans on board the ship *Creole* overpowered the crew, murdering one man, while sailing from Hampton Roads, Virginia, to New Orleans, Louisiana. Led by Madison Washington, they sailed the vessel to Nassau, Bahamas, where the British declared most of them free.

In the diplomatic controversy that followed, Ohio Congressman Joshua Giddings argued that once the ship was outside of U.S. territorial waters, the African Americans were entitled to their liberty and that any attempt to re-enslave them would be unconstitutional. Censured by the House of Representatives, he resigned, but his constituents quickly re-elected him and sent him back to Congress.

Slavery in the Western Hemisphere lasted for 348 years – from 1517 to 1865. The years following 1865, in the United States in particular, were treacherous and devastating for Black men, women and children. There

were **100 years of post-slavery lynching, in addition to rape, genocide, castration, racism and innumerable other injustices.**

So here we are near the end of 2012 (as of this writing), living in a country built on the backs of slaves who gave three-and-a-half centuries of free slave labor. Every one of them had a job, but not one of them ever had a pay day. In 2012 our future as a race still looks very, very bleak.

The next and final chapter of this book, *The Forcing of A 'Strange Religion' Upon Our Enslaved Foreparents,* will deal with one of the major problems which still has us mentally, emotionally and psychologically enslaved as a people. ENOUGH IS ENOUGH!

Chapter 12

THE FORCING OF A *STRANGE RELIGION* UPON OUR ENSLAVED FOREPARENTS

"OH THAT MY HEAD WERE WATERS, and mine eyes a fountain of tears, that I might weep day and night for the slain of the daughter of my people!" (Jeremiah 9:1.)

At the bottom of the Atlantic Ocean lie the bones of countless millions of African men, women and children. From ca. 1517 to 1808 – more than 300 years worth of bones! These are the bones of the innumerable host who perished in the Middle Passage. It is necessary to note here that after 1808 it was illegal to export Africans as slaves, but for several decades after, the Slave Trade continued.

No! Remembrance of the stigma, sting and stench of the worse crime ever perpetrated upon a people throughout the history of mankind is not going away. That's much of the problem: The Black race has been too forgiving and forgetting, to its own detriment – forgiving everyone but each other.

We see the talk shows on TV; we hear them on radio. Many African Americans call and say, "Black people ought to just forget about slavery; that was over a 150 years ago." The hearts of those of us who love our people bleed. It cuts like a knife. Don't kid yourself; we are still suffering from what was inflicted upon us during the centuries of slavery. Most of all and worst of all, we are suffering from a slave mentality. The chains are now on our minds. No amount of money could be paid to European Jews anywhere in the world to forget about their holocaust under Hitler's Germany. And this is as it should be.

More than 3,500 years ago Black Egyptians enslaved Black Hebrews. Of the 39 books which comprise the Old Testament canon, 29 of them mention the Egyptian bondage and the Israelites' deliverance in some way. The Almighty never meant for Israel to ever forget their 430-year sojourn in Egypt, their bitter, rigorous slavery, or His mighty power demonstrated in their deliverance. Hence, tens of thousands of people of the Judaic persuasion the world over – Black, Brown, Yellow and White – observe Passover annually to this day. A behest from the LORD God of Israel, as recorded in Exodus 12:14, reads: "And this day shall be unto you for a memorial; and ye shall keep it a feast to the LORD throughout your generations: and ye shall keep it a feast by an ordinance for ever."

After more than 3,500 years the Egyptian experience has been repeated, this time in England, the Americas, the Caribbean, Central America, etc., with England, Portugal and Spain being the major (but not the only) players in the drama of the African Slave Trade. The constant kidnapping, selling and buying of Black flesh went unchallenged for nearly 350 years. Between 50- and 100-million descendants of the aboriginal man were chained and dragged from the western and southern shores of the Mother Continent over the three centuries, packed like sardines in a can aboard slave ships, and brought to the so-called New World – new to the slave trafficker but not to the Native American who had lived there from time immemorial. African mariners, too, had for centuries before sailed the waters of the Atlantic and visited these 'New World' lands, as attested to in the scholarly book by Dr. Ivan Van Sertima, *They Came Before Columbus.*

The object of this chapter is not to give a detailed account of slavery and all its abominableness (as all the books ever written could never accomplish that), but its main purpose is to focus on the forcing of that "Strange Religion" upon each and every one of the tens of millions of slaves who lived to reach the shores of their new habitation.

Destroy a people's awareness of its God, and you destroy a people – when you fail to put something better in its place. The African was well aware of the existence of the Creator – the one Divine Unseen Spirit Being – interpreted out of their various languages and dialects into English as "THE GREAT ONE." But when they reached these and other shores, a new and strange religion – Christianity – was whipped and beat into them, and a new god – Jesus – was forced upon them. This Jesus did not look like the African that he really was, but was Caucasian like their oppressor, with long, silky, blonde hair, blue eyes, and carrying a white lamb.

After the first few generations of slaves died out, each succeeding one knew less and less of the old African way. Thus the slavemaster's religion was cruelly hammered into the African slave.

There are many arguments in support of the forcing of this strange religion upon our enslaved foreparents. The most popular of them says, "This was God's way of civilizing the Black man and bringing him into the knowledge of Jesus Christ and Christianity." Nigeria, Senegal, Togo, Dahomey, the Ivory and Gold Coasts, Liberia and many other West African countries were already civilized, had their own African kingdoms, and not a few of them were reigning as kings, queens, princes and princesses before the European invasions. As far as "bringing the African into the knowledge of Jesus Christ and Christianity" is concerned, Jesus (whose real name was not Jesus, but Yeshua ben Yosef) never heard the name "Jesus" nor the title "Christ"; neither was he the founder of Christianity, though all of Christendom, the encyclopædia, and many, but not all, European Jewish writers may differ.

Easter, Christmas, Sunday worship, Pentecost, the Gregorian (Roman) Calendar and the Cross were all completely foreign to and undeard of by the people of the regions from whence the Africans were stolen away; but where the Islamic influence had not snuffed it out sword-wise, the biblical Sabbath and many other Hebraic tenets were very much practiced in much of Black Africa.

Consider the Essentialness of the Following

Of all the bondages, captivities and servitudes that ancient Israel in biblical times was repeatedly thrust into and delivered out of – beginning with the Egyptian bondage under the Pharoahs – there was not one instance where Israel's God Yahweh ever sanctioned their worship of the oppressor's god or gods, or their pursuing of the oppressor's idolatrous customs and traditions.

Do you think that a just God – whom the Scriptures bespeak as "righteous in all His ways, and holy in all His works" – would allow the cruel, wicked abominable slavemaster to give us the TRUE Religion? The Most High would never allow that manner of person or group of persons to even be guardians of the TRUE Religion. Think about it, Black Man! I'm talking about the man who stole, chained, bought, sold, raped, castrated, burned, flogged, flayed, separated, renamed, destroyed, distressed and diseased our forefathers, -mothers, and their sons and daughters – not only then, but even now! I ask you again: Would a Just God . . .?

The opposition could easily counter: Would God allow the

same cruel man to thrust the African into captivity, bondage and rigorous servitude for nearly 350 years?

And the answer is: Yes! just as He suffered the ancient Egyptians, the Assyrians, the Babylonians, and , in later times the Greeks and Romans, to oppress the Israelites of yester-century. And in every case the Almighty demonstrated His awesome power in behalf of the downtrodden. Sometimes it takes years, decades and even centuries; other times it may happen overnight; but in the end, Right will prevail, and the Truth that has been crushed to the earth will rise again.

Hidden Meaning in Some "Negro" Spirituals

Although the slaves could no longer practice their culture and religion upon reaching this hemisphere, they kept a certain song in their souls, and that certain song in their souls kept them. This category of music known as Negro Spirituals releases a 400-year secret that has almost been entirely overlooked; to wit: A large number of these Spirituals tell of the slaves' apparent former connection to the ancient biblical people, places and events. Among the earliest Spirituals were those such as "Rock My Soul in the Bosom of Abraham," "Didn't It Rain!" (from Noah and the Flood), "We Are Climbing Jacob's Ladder," "Go Down, Moses," "Joshua Fit de Battle of Jericho," "Little David, Play On Your Harp," "There Is a Balm in Gilead," (from the Book of Jeremiah), "Roll, Jordan, Roll," "Deep River, My Home is Over Jordan," "Didn't Ol' Pharoah Get Lost in That Red Sea!" "Shadrach, Meshach and Abed-nego," "Did't My God Deliver Daniel, and I Know He Will Deliver Me," and many more. It would be totally absurd to hint or suggest that the slavemaster had anything whatsoever to do with the teaching of this beautiful and glorious music to our forebears.

Then there was yet another type of Spiritual which the slaves sang that was strictly a code, or escape, song. One of them is entitled "Steal Away To Jesus." This song had no reference at all to Jesus of Nazareth, but spoke, in code, of the slave ship *Jesus* on which thousands of slaves had crossed the Atlantic Ocean.

Listen to the words, then let us resurrect their original meaning:

-CHORUS -

Steal away, steal away, steal away to Jesus;
Steal away, steal away home –
I ain't got long to stay here.

DECODE: *Steal away,* very quietly, from the plantation to the Jesus Ship. *Steal away home:* Let's steal the ship and go back home – across the Atlantic to Africa. *I ain't got long to stay here:* The ill and humane treatment is intolerable; I must leave this awful land and people before long.

- Verse I –

My Lord, He calls me, He calls me by the thunder;
The trumpet sounds within my soul –
I ain't got long to stay here.

DECODE: We will plan our escape during a heavy rainstorm. While it is thundering and lightning, let's run to the ship. *The trumpet sounds within my soul:* Something inside of my soul keeps urging me, urging me, urging me to run away from this horrible place.

- VERSE II –

Green trees are bending, poor sinner stands a-trembling,
The trumpet sounds within my soul –
I ain't got long to stay here.

DECODE: *Green trees are bending:* The storm is so fierce and the wind so high that the trees are bending over. *Poor sinner stands a-trembling:* The escaping slave calls himself a "poor sinner." He says, "I'm tremblingly afraid! Will I successfully escape? Or will I be caught, whipped, even killed? Howbeit, the trumpet within my soul sounds: 'Run! Run! Run! to the Jesus Ship.'"

Another escape song used by the slaves was "Wade In the Water": *Wade in the water, wade in the water, children;*
   Wade in the water, my God's gonna trouble de water.

The Black Church

What is known today as "the Black Church" has really been a pillar of strength and a bulwark of protection for people of African ancestry, especially during the years of slavery and the ones immediately following. There are many other predominantly Black religious institutions which do not categorize themselves as being a part of "the Black Church," per sé, but which have also been "as a hiding place from the wind, as a shelter from the storm, and as a shadow of a great rock in a weary land."

As painful as it may sometimes be, the truth must be told. There is a striking similarity between Martin Luther and his followers' separation from the Roman Catholic Church in 1520, and Richard Allen and his band of supporters who left the segregated gallery of St. George Methodist Church in 1787, which was the beginning of "the Black Church."

When Luther denounced Catholicism and became the father of Lutheranism, he continued to hold on to most of the same doctrines which the Catholic Church had instituted during its 1100-year existence. Such doctrines as Christmas, Sunday as the Lord's Day, Palm Sunday, Good Friday, Easter, Pentecost, etc., are all a part of the Lutheran Church and most other Protestant churches to this day, though Jesus, whom

Christianity has adopted as its founder, was completely ignorant of any of the above man-ordained celebrations.

Likewise, when Allen had his fill of the White Methodists' segregation policy, he established the African Methodist Episcopal Church (A.M.E.). The fact cannot be negated that the parent Methodist Church had its genesis in England, and was founded by a Caucasian, John Wesley (1703-1791). The same false doctrines, therefore, which had been forced upon our foreparents in slavery were carried over into the new A.M.E. Church. All Protestantism throughout the world – Black, White or otherwise – is obeying the authority of the Roman Catholic Church, the only major difference being that the Pope of Rome is not its temporal and spiritual head.

Then Came the Christian Missionaries

Shortly after the Civil War the Christian missionaries swarmed into western and southern Africa like bees, carrying this "strange religion" to the remnant of the Slave Trade. By now, those sections of Africa were "on their knees," and the remnant consisted mostly of the poor and unlearned. Some food, some clothing and many deceitful smiles; lots of Christian songs and lots of pictures and lies about the Caucasian Jesus, under the guise of showing the natives a more excellent way, were the methods used by the missionaries to nudge their way into the hearts and souls of the remnant. The African had the land, and the White missionary had the New Testament. But before long, the African had the New Testament and the missionary had the land. The indigenous people had to bend, buckle and bow in order to survive.

Of the tens of millions who left Africa during those three centuries of exportation, not one of them was a Christian! There were, however, millions of Black Hebrews (Jews), as little as it is known, who endured the Middle Passage. Steven

S. Jacobs, a European Jew, fully documents this fact in his book, *The Hebrew Heritage of Black Africa.*† The late Professor Joseph Williams of Boston College, a Caucasian author, has also written exclusively on the subject in his more than 400-page book, *The Hebrewisms of West Africa.*††

Conclusion

The author realizes how painful a topic *The Forcing of A Strange Religion Upon Our Enslaved Foreparents* is, but trusts that the reader will bear in mind that the object of this chapter – and the entire book – is not to offend, but to enlighten.

In this chapter a brief overview has been given of how the enslaved Africans – against their will – arrived in this hemisphere, and that discussion has been coupled with mention of the more than three centuries of inhumane treatment.

The sustaining power of both Almighty God and the Negro Spirituals during those "cloudy and gloomy" days has also been highlighted, and "Steal Away To Jesus" has been deciphered.

Striking comparisons have been made between Martin Luther's separation from Catholicism and Richard Allen's from the parent Methodist Church, making clear how our progenitors, in most cases through brute force, became Christianized.

Lastly, the White Christian missionaries' arrival into Africa during post-Civil War years has been pointed out, as well as some of the tactics used by them to convert the remnant.

Truly, it has been well said by the Most High, through the mouth of the Prophet Hosea, *"My people are destroyed for lack of knowledge.*

---

† "The Hebrew Heritage of Black Africa," by Steven S. Jacobs. 128 pp. Send $16.00 + $3.25 S&H: total: $19.25. Mail to: Moses Farrar, P.O. Box 3911, Philadelphia, PA 19146.

†† "The Hebrewisms of West Africa," by Joseph Williams. Public Library.

SUMMARY

WE HAVE STRIVEN vehemently in this book to re-establish the eternal truths promulgated by the biblical prophets from Abraham through Jesus. It is hoped that this work will be an instrument by which the thinking and belief of millions will be reversed, and that they will come into the knowledge of the Truth. "Truth" is a great virtue, and is one of the three feet on which the world stands, the other two being "Justice" and "Mercy." Moses proclaims the Almighty as *"a God of Truth."* Jesus declares that Freedom comes through the knowledge of Truth: *"...And ye shall know the truth, and the truth shall make you free."*

Many the world over are unaware of the fact that a Nicene Council of 325 C.E. (A.D.) ever even existed, let alone what it did to overthrow and destroy the holy and righteous way established by the Most High through His prophets over the previous 2,200 years.

We have also herein identified the nations of antiquity mentioned in the Old Testament Scriptures (many of which are listed in Genesis chapter 10) as being of the Black race, and have concluded that (1) Abraham, Moses and Yeshua (Jesus) sprang from this race of people, and that (2) the Bible is a "Black History" book. The multitude of contributions to civilization made by the descendants of Ham and Shem have been and remain to be a blessing to the entire world.

We have destroyed the myth that "the entire Black race is the curse of Ham," and hopefully have helped to repair and restore the self esteem of our people.

The "Pauline Jesus" as set forth by an over-zealous Apostle Paul during the last half of the first century, and continued by the early Gentile Church fathers through the fifth century, has been replaced by a "better and truer Jesus" – the Yeshua (Jesus) whom he would recognize were he on earth today. This book clearly proclaims that the Almighty Creator alone is the Most High, and beside Him there is none other, and with Him there is no equal.

The Adam and Eve story has been grossly misunderstood and mis-interpreted. We have attempted to show through Scripture and common sense that all men are not sinners because of Adam's transgression, hence the Doctrine of Original Sin is unacceptable.

The last chapter in this book deals with "our Holocaust" over nearly 500 years – which still hasn't fully ended – and how our fore-parents, as slaves, were forced to accept a new and strange religion.

God still cries out through the teaching of His prophets, "Return unto Me, for I have redeemed thee."

107

BIBLIOGRAPHY

CHURCHWARD, ALBERT. *The Origin and Evolution of the Human Race.* London: George Allen and Unwin, 1921.

DAVIDSON, BASIL. *A Guide to African History.* Garden City, N.Y.: Doubleday and Co., 1965.

DIOP, CHEIKH ANTA. *The African Origin of Civilization: Myth or Reality.* West Port, Connecticut: Lawrence Hill and Co., 1974.

GODBEY, ALLEN H. *The Lost Tribes A Myth:* Durham, N.C.: Duke University Press, 1930.

HUGHLEY, ELLA J. *The Truth About Black Biblical Hebrew Israelites:* Hughley Publications, POB 130261, Springfield Gardens, NY 11413.
_____. *Awake! Awake! Black Man – Reclaim Your Legacy.* Springfield Gardens, NY. Hughley Publications. 1983. An inspirational poem portrayed on a poster with images of ancient Africans.

JACOBS, STEVEN. *The Hebrew Heritage of Black Africa.* Reprinted by permission, 1989, Moses Farrar, P.O. Box 3911, Phila., PA 19146.

JAMES, GEORGE G. *The Stolen Legacy.* Reprinted by U.B. & U.S. Communications Systems, 1989. Hampton, VA 23669.

JOSEPHUS, FLAVIUS. *The Great Roman-Jewish War: A.D. 66-70.* The William Whiston Translation as Revised by D.S. Margoliouth. New York, Harper and Row Publishers, Inc., 1970.

KOESTLER, ARTHUR. *The Thirteenth Tribe.* New York: Random House, 1976.

MEADE, FRANK SPENCER. *Handbook of Denominations,* 9th edition. 1990. Abingdon Press, Nashville, Tenn.

POTTER, CHARLES. *The Story of Religion.* Garden City Press, Garden City, L.I., N.Y.

ROGERS, J.A. *Nature Knows No Color Line.* Publisher: Helga M. Rogers, 4975 59th Avenue South, St. Petersburg, FL 33715.
_____. *Sex and Race.* Publisher: Helga M. Rogers, 4975 59th Avenue South, St. Petersburg, FL 33715.
_____. *World's Great Men of Colour,* Vol.1, New York: F. Hubner & Co., 1946.

WILLIAMS, JOSEPH. *Hebrewisms of West Africa.* New York: The Bible and Tannen Press, 1930.

BIBLES:

African Heritage Bible. King James Version. The James C. Winston Company, Nashville, Tenn.

The Holy Scriptures. (Masoretic Text.) Jewish Pub. Society, Philadelphia.

The Holy Bible. King James Version.

IT WILL SHOW IN YOUR FACE

You don't have to tell how you live each day,

You don't have to say if you work or you play;

A tried, true barometer serves in the place –

However you live, it will show in your face.

The false, the deceit that you wear in your heart

Will not stay inside where it first got its start;

For sinew and blood are a thin veil of lace:

What you wear in your heart, you wear in your face.

If in a great service you are now engaged,

If humanity's welfare you've always upstaged,

If you've played the game fair and you stand on first base,

You won't have to tell it, it will show in your face.

If your life is unselfish, if for others you live,

For not what you get, but how much you can give;

If you live close to God in His infinite grace,

You won't have to tell it, it will show in your face.

-- Author Unknown

ABOUT THE AUTHOR

MOSES FARRAR was born in Richmond, Virginia, and is the youngest of eight children. At the age of seven he went to live in the Hampton Roads Virginia area, 90 miles southeast of Richmond. Shortly after his arrival there he was selected from among many others in his age group to be trained in printing, where he learned to set type by hand – one letter at a time. In 1941 his mother took him to Philadelphia to live. When old enough to enter high school he chose to attend Dobbins Vocational Technical High School, where he continued studies in printing. He has worked on the staff of several newspapers and book-making plants in Philadelphia and Virginia. In 1969 he opened his own printing business in Philadelphia, operating it for eight years.

Ordained an Elder of an international Israelite congregation in 1971 (of which he is virtually a life-long member), he has headed congregations in Atlantic City, NJ, Brooklyn, NY, New Haven, CT, Rochester, NY, and Philadelphia. After moving to Brooklyn in 1976, he again established his printing business there for 15 years.

Elder Farrar is considered by many to be among the leading biblicists, biblical historians and lecturers, having presented lectures and historical and spiritual seminars since 1980 at colleges and houses of worship of various religious persuasions. In 1991 Elder Farrar lectured from the stage of the world-famous Apollo Theater in Harlem, NY. The author was chosen by the Chief Rabbi of his congregation to visit South Africa in 1991, 1992 and 1994, to assist in strengthening the spiritual work of our many associated congregations there. For 15 years he was a member of the religious panel for the training course, "Facilitating African American Adoption," sponsored by the New York Chapter Association of Black Social Workers' Adoption Service.

Shortly after the death of his beloved wife Naomi in September 2004, he moved back to Philadelphia, where he now resides.

Farrar is listed in the 2000 and forward editions of *Who's Who Among African Americans*. His book titles include: *"The Deceiving of the Black Race"; "The Hebrew Heritage of Black Africa"* (co-author);, *"A Non-Christian's Response To Christianity"; "The Hebrew Heritage of Black Africa"; "What Will It Take To Wake Us Up?"; "Lavinia My Mother, Naomi My Wife"; "Old Testament & New Testament: The Vast Differences"; "40 Most Frequently Asked Questions To Hebrew Israelites – With Answers"; "Yeshua (Jesus), Who Thought He Was the Messiah";* and *"What Black Christians Should Know (But Don't) About Christianity."*

ORDER FORM FOR BOOKS

Send check/m.o., payable to: "MOSES FARRAR"
Mail to: P.O. BOX 3911 • PHILADELPHIA, PA 19146

Telephone: (215) 545-0548

Books $16. ea. + $3.25 S&H. $1. More S&H for ea. add'l book mailed in 1 pkg.

- -

☐__ Copies, *"The Deceiving of the Black Race,"* 112 pp.

☐__ Copies, *"A Non-Christian's Response To Christianity,"* 152 pp.

☐__ Copies, *"The Hebrew Heritage of Black Africa,"* 128 pp.

☐__ Copies, *"What Will It Take To Wake Us Up?",* 76 pp.

☐__ Copies, *"Lavinia My Mother, Naomi My Wife,"* 90 pp.

☐__ Copies, *"The Hebrew Scriptures (O.T.) & The Greek Scriptures (N.T.): The Vast Differences,"* 132 p.

☐__ Copies, *"40 Most FAQs (Frequently Asked Questions) To Hebrew Israelites – With Answers,"* 88 pp.

☐__ Copies, *"Rabbi Yeshua ben Yosef (Jesus), Who Thought He Was the Messiah,"* 136 pp.

☐__ Copies, *"What Black Christians Should Know (But Don't) About Christianity,"* 136 pp.

☐__ Copies, *"Christianity: A False, Man-made Religion! The Hebrew Israelite Way: Ordained By the Creator!"* 128 pp.

Enclosed is chk./m.o. in the amt. of $_____ for above books.

NAME _____

ADDRESS _____

CITY _____ **STATE** _____ **Zip** _____

PHONE (____ **)** _____

Email _____ (I need it, please.)

111

-   *Notes*   -

~